Chinese Investments in Southeast Asia

T0413389

Chinese Investments in Southeast Asia

Patterns and Significance

EVELYN GOH • LIU NAN

 YUSOF ISHAK INSTITUTE

Published by: ISEAS Publishing
                 30 Heng Mui Keng Terrace
                 Singapore 119614
                 publish@iseas.edu.sg
                 http://bookshop.iseas.edu.sg

The responsibility for facts and opinions in this publication rests exclusively with the authors and their interpretations do not necessarily reflect the views or the policy of the publisher or its supporters.

ISEAS Library Cataloguing-in-Publication Data

Name(s): Goh, Evelyn, author. | Liu, Nan, author.
Title: Chinese investments in Southeast Asia : patterns and significance / by Evelyn Goh and Liu Nan.
Description: Singapore : ISEAS-Yusof Ishak Institute, 2023. | Includes bibliographical references and index.
Identifiers: ISBN 9789815104578 (soft cover) | ISBN 9789815104585 (ebook PDF)
Subjects: LCSH: Investments, Chinese—Southeast Asia. | China—Foreign relations—Southeast Asia. | Southeast Asia—Foreign relations—China.
Classification: LCC HG5740.8 A3G61

Cover photo: Dam Construction for Energy Supply in the Lower Reaches of the Nam Ou River (CC BY-SA 3.0)
Image by Tbachner on Wikimedia Commons.

Cover design by Lee Meng Hui
Typeset by Superskill Graphics Pte Ltd
Index compiled by Raffaie Nahar
Printed in Singapore by Markono Print Media Pte Ltd

CONTENTS

LIST OF FIGURES

LIST OF TABLES

ACKNOWLEDGEMENTS

The authors are grateful for the feedback, advice, and support from colleagues and friends, including Dr Alexander Chandra, Professor Paul Hutchcroft, Dr Andy Kennedy, Dr Hasnani Rangkuti, Dr Derek Scissors, Dr Jonathan Stromseth, Professor Andrew Walter, and Professor Wang Gungwu. At the Australian National University (ANU), we thank Dr Elly Kent for facilitating the initial dissemination of our brief findings in *New Mandala*, and Mr Emirza Adi Syailendra for his valuable research assistance. At the ISEAS – Yusof Ishak Institute, we are indebted to Dr Terence Chong, Mr Ng Kok Kiong, and Ms Rahilah Yusuf for their warm support and professionalism. The work for this study was supported by two research grants: the Australian Research Council Discovery Project on "The Infrastructure of China's Influence" (DP190100755), and Phase II of the "Supporting the Rules-Based Order in Southeast Asia" Project at the ANU.

EXECUTIVE SUMMARY

- Southeast Asia's growing economic linkages and dependence on China for investment in infrastructure and industry have generated political opportunities and strategic concerns in equal measure.
- How much has Chinese investment grown in Southeast Asia in the past two decades, and how significant is this increase? How does Chinese investment compare to other sources of investment in the region? Is it more significant in some countries than in others, or in specific sectors more than others? What are the political and strategic implications of growing large Chinese investments in the region?
- This project investigates the levels, trends and distribution of Chinese investment in Southeast Asia, providing an important regionwide analysis that allows comparisons and facilitates policy calibration and focus.
- The first section of the report presents an overview of its findings about the regionwide trends and key changes in large Chinese investment, outlining the distribution of Chinese investment across Southeast Asian countries and economic sectors from 2005 to 2019.
- It then explores the political and strategic significance of these Chinese investments in Southeast Asia in terms of vulnerability and dependency, and strategic integration.
- The second section of the report contains the project's detailed quantitative analysis of large Chinese investment in Southeast Asia, presented by country and by sector. This dataset can be used by others for further analysis.
- The Appendix explains the definitions, coding and other decisions made in the construction of the dataset, highlights its uses, and points out some of its limitations.

ABOUT THE AUTHORS

Evelyn GOH is the Shedden Professor of Strategic Policy Studies at the Australian National University, where she is also the Director of the Southeast Asia Institute. She has published widely on US-China relations and diplomatic history, regional order in East Asia, Southeast Asian strategies towards great powers, and environmental security. Her books include *Rising China's Influence in Developing Asia* (Oxford University Press, 2016), and (co-authored with Barry Buzan) *Rethinking Sino-Japanese Alienation: History Problems and Historical Opportunities* (Oxford University Press, 2020).

LIU Nan was a research officer for this project. She received her Master of Business Information Systems from the Australian National University's College of Business and Economics, and her Bachelor of Economics and Finance from the University of Hong Kong. She is experienced in conducting both quantitative and qualitative research in the fields of economics and strategic studies.

Section 1
OVERVIEW AND ANALYSIS

This first section provides an overview and analysis of the full Quantitative Report which follows.

Southeast Asia's growing economic linkages with and dependence on China for investment have generated political opportunities and strategic concerns in equal measure. However, recent discussions have tended to focus on infrastructure projects, especially those associated with the Belt and Road Initiative (BRI). This narrow focus can be misleading, and an understanding of the fuller picture of Chinese investments in Southeast Asia is necessary for those seeking to understand its significance and impacts. The People's Republic of China (PRC) is not a new player in this game, having had a longer history of providing investment and aid in this region, particularly in support of independence struggles and civil and regional conflicts during the Cold War.[1] After 1990 and reflecting Beijing's economic reform and internationalization strategy, Chinese investment in Southeast Asia picked up gradually across varied sectors. Prior to President Xi Jinping's unveiling in 2013 of what has come to be called BRI, Southeast Asia had already seen a turning point in the growing significance of Chinese investments during the global financial crisis in 2008/9.

This report is part of a research project that examines China's investment in Southeast Asia, aiming to provide a regionwide, multi-sectoral analysis that allows comparisons and facilitates policy calibration and focus. In this quantitative report, we present the baseline quantitative survey and analysis of key changes in Chinese investments in Southeast Asian economies over the most recent fifteen years, from 2005 to 2019, for which comparable data is available.[2]

By "investment", we refer to Chinese investment, project financing, and service provision in the region. The CGIT dataset that our report relies on captures the two key forms of Foreign Direct Investment (mergers and acquisitions, and greenfield investment), *as well as* other forms of cross-border investment flows associated with Chinese investments in Southeast Asia. Construction contracts, in particular, often accompany Chinese overseas investment and are a form of trade in services that can be even more significant than FDI.[3]

1.1 Regionwide Trends

Foreign investments in Southeast Asia (SEA) originating from China grew twentyfold during this fifteen-year period. This trend is more marked when we define foreign investments as including both ownership acquisition of specific enterprises, and service provision (such as construction contracts). As Figure 1 shows, the first phase of rapidly expanding Chinese investments in SEA occurred around 2009–12, when temporary declines in other sources of FDI following the global financial crisis coincided with Beijing's "going out" strategy encouraging international investment by domestic enterprises. The second phase of rapid increase took place between 2013 and 2017, following the official announcement of BRI, which further enabled log-rolling outward investment from multiple Chinese enterprises. Indeed, the vast majority of very large (at least US$1 billion) Chinese investments came after the advent of the BRI in 2013 for all SEA countries except Vietnam and Myanmar (as indicated in red and pink on Figure 2).

Even so, at a regionwide level, China is not yet a dominant investor. Between 2005 and 2018 China featured in the top three (non-ASEAN) foreign investors list in SEA only twice (in 2012 and 2018, both in third place—see Table 1). In each instance, China's share of SEA's total annual FDI was only half that of the second largest investor, Japan. The EU, Japan, and the United States remained the three largest sources of FDI for SEA across this period.

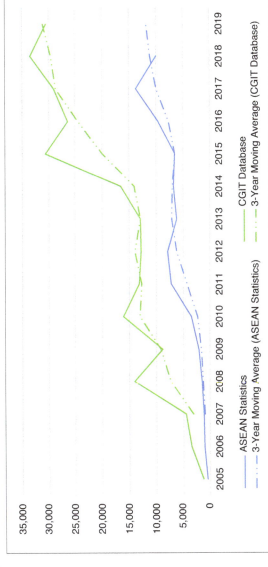

Figure 1: Chinese Investments (in US$ million) in SEA, 2005–19

Data Source: China Global Investment Tracker 2019 Fall Dataset (accessed in January 2020), China Global Investment Tracker 2021 Spring Dataset (accessed in August 2021) and ASEAN Statistical Yearbooks.

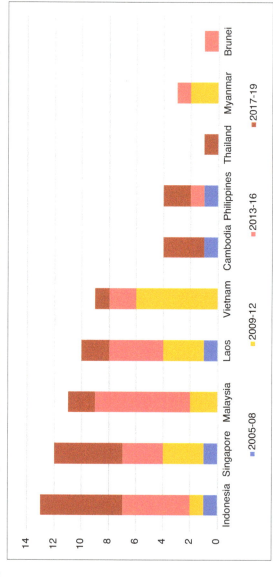

Figure 2: Number of Chinese Investments Worth at Least US$1 billion in SEA Countries, 2005–19

Data Source: China Global Investment Tracker 2019 Fall Dataset (accessed in January 2020), China Global Investment Tracker 2021 Spring Dataset (accessed in August 2021) and ASEAN Statistical Yearbooks.

Table 1: Top Three (Non-ASEAN) Foreign Investors in SEA, 2005–18

Year	Total	Largest Investor			Second Largest Investor			Third Largest Investor			Chinese FDI to SEA (in US$ million)	
		Investor	Amount	Share	Investor	Amount	Share	Investor	Amount	Share	Amount	Share
2005	39,629	EU	10,016	25%	Japan	6,655	17%	US	3,946	10%	538	1%
2006	54,967	EU	10,672	19%	Japan	10,223	19%	US	3,406	6%	1,016	2%
2007	69,482	EU	18,384	26%	Japan	8,382	12%	US	6,346	9%	1,227	2%
2008	60,596	EU	12,445	21%	Japan	7,654	13%	US	3,393	6%	1,497	2%
2009	43,365	EU	5,660	13%	US	5,181	12%	Japan	3,451	8%	2,069	5%
2010	108,174	EU	21,145	20%	US	13,682	13%	Japan	12,987	12%	3,489	3%
2011	87,563	EU	24,419	28%	US	8,197	9%	Japan	7,798	9%	7,194	8%
2012	116,774	US	18,911	16%	Japan	14,853	13%	China	7,975	7%	7,975	7%
2013	120,966	Japan	24,609	20%	EU	15,719	13%	US	11,458	9%	6,165	5%
2014	130,115	EU	28,943	22%	US	21,141	16%	Japan	13,436	10%	6,812	5%
2015	118,667	US	22,913	19%	EU	20,373	17%	Japan	12,962	11%	6,572	6%
2016	118,960	EU	34,015	29%	US	21,663	18%	Japan	14,242	12%	9,610	8%
2017	147,085	US	24,891	17%	Japan	16,149	11%	EU	14,916	10%	13,701	9%
2018	152,755	EU	21,614	14%	Japan	20,955	14%	China	9,940	7%	9,940	7%

Data Source: ASEAN Statistical Yearbooks.

Within these limitations, however, China has diversified its SEA investments across industrial sectors as well as host countries, laying a broader-based foundation for the potential impacts and influence of Chinese investment in the region. As Figure 3 demonstrates, from an earlier investment profile resting heavily on the energy sector in 2005–10, Chinese investments significantly diversified in scope in 2011–19, doubling in infrastructure, metals and in the *other* sector. In particular, the infrastructure sector's average share of total Chinese investments in the latter period rose to 30 per cent, slightly lower than the leading energy sector's 35 per cent share. The domain of Chinese investments also expanded: in 2005–7, they barely covered half the SEA countries and were concentrated significantly in Indonesia; but from 2008 these were spread across all ten SEA countries, with at least 70 per cent receiving large Chinese investments every year. China's growing SEA investment footprint results from greatly increased mobilizable Chinese capital as well as the proliferation of investment opportunities offered by the diverse SEA economies having undergone different stages of transition and development.

1.2 Distribution of Chinese Investments in SEA

It would be a mistake to regard all Chinese investments to be of one type. SEA is a large and varied political-economic landscape, and Chinese state-owned and private investors have pursued different purposes—commercial, political, strategic—when making large investments in this neighbouring region. At the same time, SEA states and political and business actors have courted Chinese investments to fulfil combinations of goals related to power and profit, to different extents and with varying results.

Table 2 presents a summary outlining the relative distribution of Chinese investments across the ten SEA countries in 2005–19 and highlights key features and examples of these investments in each country.[4]

Using the volume-based distribution of Chinese investments, SEA countries can be categorized into three groups (Figure 4).

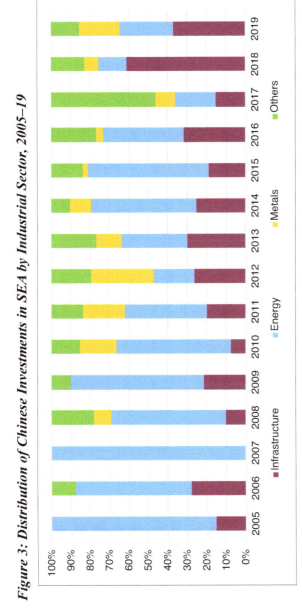

Figure 3: Distribution of Chinese Investments in SEA by Industrial Sector, 2005–19

Data Source: China Global Investment Tracker 2019 Fall Dataset (accessed in January 2020), China Global Investment Tracker 2021 Spring Dataset (accessed in August 2021) and ASEAN Statistical Yearbooks.

Table 2: Summary of Chinese Investments in Each SEA Country, 2005–19

SEA Country	Chinese Investments during 2005–19		Key Features of Chinese Investments	Major Chinese Projects	No. of Projects Worth at Least US$100 million	Of Which Projects Worth at Least US$1 billion
	Amount (in US$ million)	Share				
Indonesia	53,720	21%	– Generally increasing trend during 2005–19 – Rising relative importance of Chinese FDI in Indonesia after the global financial crisis – Primarily in the energy sector, with diversification towards the infrastructure and metals sectors after the global financial crisis	– Tanjung Jati Ultra Supercritical Clean Coal Power Station project – Jakarta-Bandung high-speed railway project – South Kalimantan steel project	117	13 (11%)
Singapore	46,310	18%	– Primarily acquisition of asset ownership during 2005–19 – Generally the third largest source of FDI in Singapore during 2005–18 (following the EU and US) – Significant shift from the energy and infrastructure sectors to other sectors (e.g., logistics and consumer sectors) since 2011	– Acquisitions of ownership in Tuas Power – Singapore Petroleum Company – Singapore Aircraft Leasing Enterprise – Global Logistic Properties – Lazada (e-commerce company)	90	12 (13%)

| Malaysia | 43,060 | 17% | – Roughly a bell-shaped pattern during 2005–19
– Increased relative importance of Chinese FDI in Malaysia after the official launch of Beijing's BRI
– Diversified across industrial sectors both in each individual year and across time during 2005–19 | – Acquisition of 1MDB's energy assets
– East Coast Rail Link project
– Perwaja Steel project | 88 | 11 (13%) |
| Laos | 28,650 | 11% | – Significant fluctuations prior to 2012 but generally increasing trend between 2012 and 2018
– Generally the largest source of FDI in Laos since 2009, with significant shares in 2011 and 2014–18
– Mainly in the energy sector, with sizeable infrastructure investments during 2015–18 | – Pak Lay hydropower dam project
– Nam Ngum 5 Hydropower project
– Nam Ou River Cascade Hydropower project
– Hongsha Coal Power plant
– Kunming-Vientiane Railway project | 51 | 10 (20%) |

continued on next page

Table 2 — cont'd

SEA Country	Chinese Investments during 2005–19		Key Features of Chinese Investments	Major Chinese Projects	No. of Projects Worth at Least US$100 million	Of Which Projects Worth at Least US$1 billion
	Amount (in US$ million)	Share				
Vietnam	25,500	10%	– Primarily service provision by Chinese entities during 2005–19 – Modest increase in the relative importance of Chinese FDI in Vietnam since 2013 (notably during 2016–18) – Mainly in the energy sector (in particular, in the coal sector)	– Offshore thermal power plant in Tra Vinh – Two coal-fired plants in Hai Duong – Vinh Tan 1 power plant in Binh Thuan – Integrated steel mill project in Ha Tinh	50	9 (18%)
Cambodia	16,240	6%	– Substantial increase since 2016 – Largest source of FDI in Cambodia during 2005–18 (except in 2008 and 2009), with considerable shares – Shift from the energy sector mainly to the infrastructure sector since 2015	– Phnom Penh-Sihanoukville Expressway project – Two coal-fired power units in Sihanoukville – Steel plant and industrial zone in Preah Vihear – Tourism resort project in Koh Kong by Tianjin Union Development Group	41	4 (10%)

| Philippines | 15,290 | 6% | – Generally increasing trend since 2016
– Insignificant source of FDI in the Philippines during 2005–18
– Predominantly in the energy sector, with increasing investments in the infrastructure sector since 2016 and significant investments in the metals sector in 2019 | – Acquisition of ownership in National Grid Corporation of the Philippines
– Thermal facility in Kauswagan
– Coal-fired power plant in Dinginin
– Investment in Mislatel (telecommunications service provider)
– Integrated steel plant in Misamis Oriental | 26 | 4
(15%) |
| Thailand | 11,550 | 5% | – Relatively stable trend during 2005–19 (apart from a spike in 2018)
– Generally low relative importance of Chinese FDI in Thailand during 2005–18
– Shift from the others sector (e.g., property and consumer sectors) to the infrastructure sector since 2012 | – Thailand-China railway project
– Acquisition of ownership in True Corp (telecoms group)
– High-Speed Rail Linking Three Airports project
– Highly automated solar module and cell manufacturing facilities in Rayong | 34 | 1
(3%) |

continued on next page

Table 2 — cont'd

SEA Country	Chinese Investments during 2005–19		Key Features of Chinese Investments	Major Chinese Projects	No. of Projects Worth at Least US$100 million	Of Which Projects Worth at Least US$1 billion
	Amount (in US$ million)	Share				
Myanmar	9,600	4%	– Primarily acquisition of asset ownership during 2008–10 and 2016–18 – Among the top three sources of FDI in Myanmar during 2005–18, with significant shares during 2008–13 – Relatively diversified across industrial sectors over time during 2005–19 but substantially concentrated in one sector in a single year	– Kyaukphyu oil-gas pipeline project – Oil refinery project in Dawei – Deep-sea port project at Kyaukphyu – Tagaung Taung Nickel Mine project – Letpadaung Copper Mine project	22	3 (14%)
Brunei	4,110	2%	– Sporadic pattern during 2005–19 (concentrated mainly in 2014) – Insignificant source of FDI in Brunei during 2005–18 – Predominantly in the energy sector	– Oil refinery and petrochemical complex project at Pulau Muara Besar – Sultan Haji Omar Ali Saifuddien Bridge project	4	1 (25%)

SEA	254.030	– *General upward trend during 2005–19* – *Moderate increase in the relative importance of Chinese FDI in SEA since 2011* – *Diversification not only across industrial sectors (since 2011) but also across SEA host countries (since 2008)*

Data Source: China Global Investment Tracker 2019 Fall Dataset (accessed in January 2020), China Global Investment Tracker 2021 Spring Dataset (accessed in August 2021).

Figure 4: Distribution of Chinese Investments in SEA by Country, 2005–19

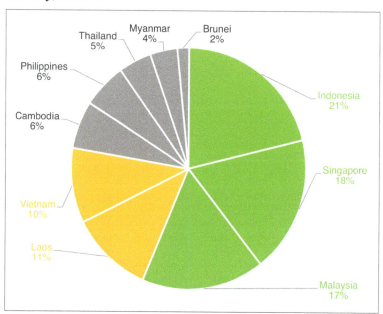

Data Source: China Global Investment Tracker 2019 Fall Dataset (accessed in January 2020), China Global Investment Tracker 2021 Spring Dataset (accessed in August 2021) and ASEAN Statistical Yearbooks.

(a) Indonesia, Singapore, Malaysia

These three key maritime SEA economies were the top three destinations, together accounting for 56 per cent of total Chinese investments in SEA.

Over the whole period, Indonesia retained its position as the top SEA destination for Chinese investments even though its share fell from 58 per cent in 2005–7 to 19 per cent in 2008–19. With the global financial crises, the Chinese investment profile in Indonesia switched from an initial concentration in service provision to include ownership acquisitions, coinciding with the relative decline of FDI from traditional external investors like the

US and EU, in 2009–13. After the official launch of Beijing's BRI, Chinese investments in Indonesia more than quadrupled from roughly US$2 billion in 2013 to US$8.6 billion in 2015, and from 2014, China ranked consistently among the top three external investors in Indonesia. Chinese investments also diversified across the energy, infrastructure and metals sectors. Much political attention has been paid to large infrastructure projects like the US$7.2 billion Jakarta-Bandung Highspeed Rail,[5] and indeed this sector attracted a fifth of total Chinese investments. However, the energy sector accounted for the bulk—around 53 per cent—of Chinese investments, mainly in coal and hydropower projects.

Singapore is the second largest recipient of Chinese investments in SEA according to the China Global Investment Tracker (CGIT) database we used for this project, garnering roughly the same amount as Malaysia. As the region's most attractive foreign investment destination by a long way, Singapore enjoys a wide variety of foreign investors and it is possible that Singapore's share of Chinese investments is higher than this, especially if all forms of indirectly routed Chinese investments could be taken into account. Within the SEA context, the city-state is a singular case because of its economic profile, which leans towards specialist heavy industries, finance and services. Chinese investment patterns were punctuated by major acquisitions reflecting Chinese corporate interest in acquiring several strategic service providers. For example, in 2008–9, Chinese consortiums spent over US$5 billion on one of the island's three electricity generation companies (Tuas Power) and the Singapore Petroleum Company when the sector was privatized. But the lion's share of Chinese investments from 2013 went into services: Alibaba's acquisition and investment in Lazada, a Singaporean e-commerce company, pumped US$4 billion into the island's economy in 2016–18; while in 2017, Chinese investments hit a record high when a Chinese consortium paid US$9 billion for Singapore-listed Global Logistic Properties, the largest warehouse operator in Asia.

Ranking third overall, Malaysia joined the top three SEA recipients in 2008, but is an unusual case for two reasons. First, the pattern of Chinese investments is dramatic, spiking around a few very major investments (Figure 5). For instance, the record high level of Chinese investments in 2015 was due to one cross-border transaction valued at US$5.26 billion: the acquisition by China General Nuclear Power Group of all energy assets owned by 1Malaysia Development Berhad (1MDB). From the second-highest level of US$6.5 billion in 2016 (centred on the East Coast Rail Link [ECRL] project), Chinese investments then decreased sharply, plunging to a record low of US$1.8 billion by 2019. This was partly due to the massive 1MDB corruption scandal, which also caused other FDI from traditional foreign investors to decline. Second, due to domestic politics—changes in central government, federal-state disagreements, and land acquisition delays—large Chinese investments in Malaysia have had a low rate of realization, especially in the infrastructure sector. Apart from the much-publicized suspension and renegotiation of the ECRL project in 2018, other major Chinese-invested projects in Mersing Laguna and Melaka Gateway were also cancelled. While not Chinese-funded, the Kuala Lumpur-Singapore Highspeed Rail, cancelled in 2020, will also have further negative implications for existing Chinese investments elsewhere in the country.[6]

(b) Laos and Vietnam

These two SEA economies each attracted around 11 per cent—together accounting for just over a fifth—of all Chinese investments in SEA.

As might be expected, these two mainland neighbours received significant portions of Chinese investment in 2005–19, notably in the energy sector—mainly hydropower in Laos, and coal in Vietnam. Laos also received sizeable Chinese infrastructure investment in 2016–18 for the railway connecting Kunming and Vientiane, part of the larger north-south regional network supported by ASEAN and BRI connectivity initiatives (Figure 6). Both Vietnam and Laos saw larger than regional average proportions of high-value (> US$1 billion) Chinese projects—18 per cent and 20 per cent

Figure 5: Chinese Investments in Malaysia (in US$ million), 2005–19

Data Source: China Global Investment Tracker 2019 Fall Dataset (accessed in January 2020), China Global Investment Tracker 2021 Spring Dataset (accessed in August 2021) and ASEAN Statistical Yearbooks.

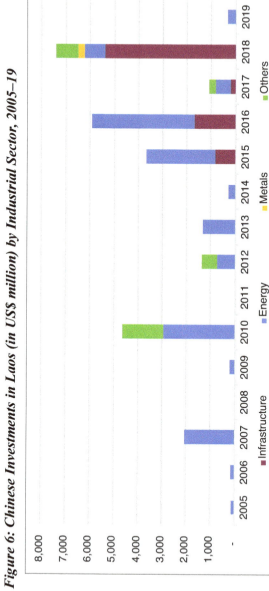

Figure 6: Chinese Investments in Laos (in US$ million) by Industrial Sector, 2005–19

Data Source: China Global Investment Tracker 2019 Fall Dataset (accessed in January 2020), China Global Investment Tracker 2021 Spring Dataset (accessed in August 2021) and ASEAN Statistical Yearbooks.

respectively—with patterns of Chinese investment driven by a few clearly identifiable high-value acquisitions or contracts. For example, the two clear peaks in Chinese investments in Vietnam (see Figure 7) were tied to one thermal power plant in 2010, and two coal plant-related investments in 2015. Such large investments similarly marked the energy sector in Laos, where major Chinese-backed hydropower projects include Pak Lay (US$1.7 billion), Nam Ngum 5 (US$1 billion), and the Nam Ou cascade (US$2 billion)—projects that have generated civil society opposition and controversy. Moreover, contracts for the Kunming-Vientiane railway accounted for a quarter of Chinese investments in Laos in 2016, and more than half in 2018.

Laos experienced a sharp increase in Chinese investments between 2013 and 2018, coinciding in part with BRI, but Chinese investment in Vietnam has been on a declining trajectory since the peak in 2010. This is related to their bilateral political tensions over conflicting territorial claims in the South China Sea, with key episodes in 2011, 2012, 2014 and 2016 coinciding with troughs in received Chinese investments. Vietnam's top foreign investments originate in South Korea, Japan and the EU, but it consistently receives over 40 per cent of its FDI from other countries. By ASEAN records, the largest share of FDI in Vietnam which China achieved was 11 per cent in 2013, compared to 79 per cent in Laos (2018). Because both these countries receive significant proportions of Chinese investments in the form of service provision, they may be more dependent on Chinese investment than we are able to show here by comparing top FDI sources based on relative ownership acquisition investments alone.[7] Nevertheless, even based just on ownership investment, since 2009, Laos is one of the two SEA economies most dependent on Chinese investments (the other being Cambodia).

(c) Cambodia, Philippines, Thailand, Myanmar and Brunei

Each of these countries received 6 per cent or less, together accounting for 22 per cent, of total Chinese investments in SEA.

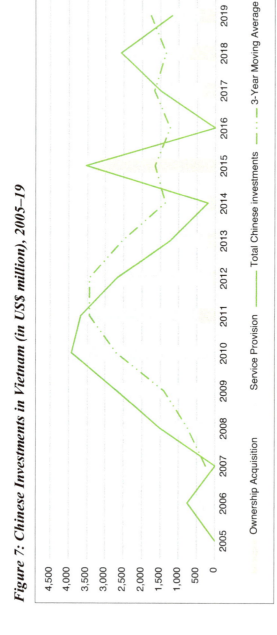

Figure 7: Chinese Investments in Vietnam (in US$ million), 2005–19

Data Source: China Global Investment Tracker 2019 Fall Dataset (accessed in January 2020), China Global Investment Tracker 2021 Spring Dataset (accessed in August 2021) and ASEAN Statistical Yearbooks.

Within this group, Cambodia and Myanmar stand out for the high significance of Chinese investment in their economies, despite the smaller amounts involved relative to the two groups above. Of all the SEA countries, Cambodia alone has consistently logged China as its top non-ASEAN FDI source in 2005–18 (except in 2008 and 2009, when it was topped by South Korea). Unlike Laos, however, Cambodia attracts a wider range of FDI and thus is less reliant on Chinese investment—for example, within the 2014–18 BRI period, China provided an average of 27 per cent of FDI in Cambodia, compared to 70 per cent in Laos (see Tables 3 and 4). Myanmar's reliance on Chinese FDI correlated with the periods of international isolation under military rule—between 2008 and 2013 especially, an average of 40 per cent of Myanmar's FDI came from China, with a peak of 68 per cent in 2010 (the year before the SPDP regime decided to undertake some political-economic reforms, partly to reduce dependence on China). That peak amount was due to a US$1.02 billion investment in the Kyaukphyu oil and gas pipeline, one of three very large Chinese investments in Myanmar, alongside the US$2.1 billion project to build Myanmar's first oil refinery in Dawei (2016), and the controversial US$1.48 billion Letpadaung open-cast copper mine (2010).

In contrast, the Philippines, Thailand and Brunei attract small proportions of Chinese investment in SEA, and also do not count China among their most significant FDI sources. The reasons vary. By a large margin, the Philippines' top foreign investor is the US (followed by Japan, the EU and South Korea), while Chinese investment is also constrained by corruption scandals and nationalist sentiment due to the South China Sea territorial disputes. Certain potentially significant Chinese investment efforts in telecommunications and electricity are discussed below. Despite its perceived economic closeness to China, Thailand's most important FDI source has been Japan (followed at some distance by the US and EU), with Chinese investment making a mark only in 2018 due to the US$2.7 billion invested for the highspeed railway connecting Thailand to China via Laos. As a major oil producer, Brunei does not have significant FDI inflows,

Table 3: Top Three (Non-ASEAN) Foreign Investors in Cambodia, 2005–18

Year	Total	Largest Investor			Second Largest Investor			Third Largest Investor			Chinese FDI to Cambodia (in US$ million)	
		Investor	Amount	Share	Investor	Amount	Share	Investor	Amount	Share	Amount	Share
2005	381	China	103	27%	S. Korea	72	19%	Australia	24	6%	103	27%
2006	483	China	130	27%	US	51	10%	S. Korea	27	6%	130	27%
2007	867	China	165	19%	S. Korea	119	14%	EU	80	9%	165	19%
2008	815	S. Korea	203	25%	China	77	9%	EU	77	9%	77	9%
2009	539	S. Korea	98	18%	China	97	18%	India	28	5%	97	18%
2010	783	China	127	16%	S. Korea	47	6%	EU	43	6%	127	16%
2011	892	China	180	20%	S. Korea	139	16%	EU	54	6%	180	20%
2012	1,557	China	368	24%	S. Korea	162	10%	EU	126	8%	368	24%
2013	1,275	China	287	22%	S. Korea	178	14%	EU	116	9%	287	22%
2014	1,727	China	554	32%	EU	139	8%	S. Korea	106	6%	554	32%
2015	1,701	China	538	32%	EU	180	11%	S. Korea	72	4%	538	32%
2016	2,280	China	502	22%	Japan	199	9%	EU	194	9%	502	22%
2017	2,732	China	618	23%	Japan	227	8%	EU	214	8%	618	23%
2018	3,103	China	798	26%	S. Korea	250	8%	Japan	199	6%	798	26%

Data Source: ASEAN Statistical Yearbooks.

Table 4: Top Three (Non-ASEAN) Foreign Investors in Laos, 2005–18

Year	Total	Largest Investor			Second Largest Investor			Third Largest Investor			Chinese FDI to Laos (in US$ million)	
		Investor	Amount	Share	Investor	Amount	Share	Investor	Amount	Share	Amount	Share
2005	28	EU	8	28%	China	5	16%	Australia	4	15%	5	16%
2006	187	EU	158	84%	China	5	3%	US	1	1%	5	3%
2007	324	Japan	18	6%	EU	15	5%	S. Korea	15	5%	2	1%
2008	228	S. Korea	47	21%	China	43	19%	EU	10	4%	43	19%
2009	319	China	36	11%	Japan	14	4%	EU	11	3%	36	11%
2010	333	China	46	14%	EU	28	8%	Japan	8	2%	46	14%
2011	467	China	278	60%	Japan	12	3%	Russia	5	1%	278	60%
2012	294					N/A					N/A	N/A
2013	427					N/A					N/A	N/A
2014	913	China	614	67%	EU	51	6%	Australia	16	2%	614	67%
2015	1,079	China	665	62%	Japan	76	7%	S. Korea	46	4%	665	62%
2016	1,076	China	710	66%	S. Korea	77	7%	Japan	44	4%	710	66%
2017	1,695	China	1,314	77%	S. Korea	102	6%	Japan	70	4%	1,314	77%
2018	1,320	China	1,045	79%	Japan	48	4%	S. Korea	25	2%	1,045	79%

Data Source: ASEAN Statistical Yearbooks.

and the few large Chinese investments in recent years are related to early efforts to diversify the Sultanate's economic base.

Looking ahead, analysts should pay attention to the first group of top three SEA recipients of Chinese investments (Indonesia, Singapore and Malaysia), because of their large existing profile and the potential for further growth in these dynamic economies attractive to Chinese capital. We should also pay heed to the third group, because of the potential to grow from the relatively low base of current Chinese investment. Myanmar and Thailand may also try to attract further Chinese investments due to constrained options arising from their relative international isolation, or investor reticence due to their military regimes.

1.3 Political and Strategic Significance

In SEA, the largest volumes and shares of Chinese investments go to the most diversified and advanced economies, while in some of the smaller developing economies, even smaller absolute amounts of investment can bring China top investor status. SEA countries with fewer options—those that are less attractive to other major international investors due to economic or political reasons— are also likely to be more dependent on Chinese investment. In assessing the political and strategic implications of Chinese investment for SEA, the findings of this report suggest a broader perspective beyond the current focus on "debt traps" surrounding a handful of controversial infrastructure loans. In particular, Chinese investments in SEA since 2005 generate dilemmas about (i) dependency and vulnerability, and (ii) strategic integration.

1.3.1 Dependency and Vulnerability

Concerns about over-dependence arise particularly in contexts where one external source of investment is of *disproportionate importance* for a national economy. China is the most important source of FDI for two SEA countries, Cambodia (every year except 2008 and 2009 when it was ranked second) and Laos (since 2009). As seen in Tables 3 and 4, Laos' relative dependence on Chinese sources is higher, reaching a peak of 79 per cent in 2018 compared to a peak of 32 per cent in Cambodia (2014 and 2015).[8] China is consistently among the top three sources of FDI for only two other SEA countries: Myanmar and Singapore. At its height, China provided 40 per cent of Myanmar's FDI in 2008–13 (Table 5). For Singapore, China is a distant third, contributing 6 per cent to its FDI in 2005–18, compared to nearly 20 per cent from the US and 25 per cent from the EU (Table 6).

Measured against their overall FDI, China has not been a leading source for the other six SEA countries, not even for Malaysia, which ranks third in terms of the volume of Chinese investments received. First-ranked Indonesia has recorded China among its top three non-ASEAN FDI sources only since 2014. Even with Vietnam—which maintains close Party-to-Party ties with the PRC and is generally one of the most popular FDI destinations in SEA alongside Singapore and Indonesia—bilateral tensions over territorial disputes meant that China only consistently retained its top-three position from 2016. On this basis, Laos, Myanmar and—to a lesser extent—Cambodia are the three SEA economies most likely to be over-exposed and potentially dependent on Chinese investments. Indeed, another recent study calculating 200 countries' vulnerability in terms of both investment and trade also found these three countries to be the most vulnerable in SEA to potential disruptions in their economic ties with China.[9]

Structural vulnerability may accompany dependence on Chinese investment, regardless of whether it involves *asset ownership* or *service provision* (a broad category in which Chinese contractors undertake activities like installation and maintenance of equipment, technical evaluation, and construction supervision). Our report shows that Chinese investments in Singapore and Myanmar largely involved ownership acquisition whereas those in Vietnam and Laos were mainly service provision, while Indonesia experienced a change from service provision to a combination of service provision and ownership acquisition between 2005 and 2019. In general, strategists have strong sovereignty concerns about foreign ownership of critical national assets—but economists

Table 5: Top Three (Non-ASEAN) Foreign Investors in Myanmar, 2005–18

Year	Total	Largest Investor			Second Largest Investor			Third Largest Investor			Chinese FDI to Myanmar (in US$ million)	
		Investor	Amount	Share	Investor	Amount	Share	Investor	Amount	Share	Amount	Share
2005	236	EU	135	57%	Australia	2	1%	China	1	1%	1	1%
2006	428	EU	181	42%	S. Korea	120	28%	China	2	0%	2	0%
2007	258	S. Korea	103	40%	EU	85	33%	China	2	1%	2	1%
2008	715	China	349	49%	EU	183	26%	S. Korea	13	2%	349	49%
2009	963	China	371	38%	EU	98	10%	NZ	65	7%	371	38%
2010	2,249	China	1,521	68%	EU	215	10%	India	14	1%	1,521	68%
2011	2,058	China	671	33%	EU	369	18%	US	103	5%	671	33%
2012	1,354	EU	664	49%	China	482	36%	Japan	31	2%	482	36%
2013	2,621	China	793	30%	EU	296	11%	Japan	36	1%	793	30%
2014	946	China	71	7%	Japan	38	4%	EU	28	3%	71	7%
2015	2,825	EU	203	7%	Japan	95	3%	China	52	2%	52	2%
2016	2,990	EU	839	28%	China	206	7%	US	43	1%	206	7%
2017	4,002	China	554	14%	EU	447	11%	Japan	208	5%	554	14%
2018	1,610	Japan	289	18%	EU	177	11%	China	75	5%	75	5%

Data Source: ASEAN Statistical Yearbooks.

Table 6: Top Three (Non-ASEAN) Foreign Investors in Singapore, 2005–18

Year	Total	Largest Investor			Second Largest Investor			Third Largest Investor			Chinese FDI to Singapore (in US$ million)	
		Investor	Amount	Share	Investor	Amount	Share	Investor	Amount	Share	Amount	Share
2005	14,373	EU	6,072	42%	Japan	1,800	13%	India	379	3%	69	0%
2006	27,681	EU	5,316	19%	Japan	3,312	12%	US	1,926	7%	617	2%
2007	31,550	EU	11,503	36%	US	2,949	9%	Japan	1,408	4%	594	2%
2008	22,802	EU	8,463	37%	Japan	1,493	7%	China	478	2%	478	2%
2009	18,917	US	3,306	17%	EU	1,336	7%	China	1,049	6%	1,049	6%
2010	57,214	EU	16,929	30%	US	6,915	12%	India	3,643	6%	699	1%
2011	39,887	EU	15,991	40%	US	6,465	16%	China	5,467	14%	5,467	14%
2012	60,102	US	13,784	23%	US	6,982	12%	China	5,970	10%	5,970	10%
2013	56,671	EU	14,313	25%	US	9,923	18%	Japan	2,662	5%	2,508	4%
2014	73,285	EU	23,878	33%	US	18,287	25%	China	4,168	6%	4,168	6%
2015	59,702	US	17,784	30%	EU	15,266	26%	China	3,991	7%	3,991	7%
2016	73,864	EU	32,336	44%	US	18,941	26%	China	4,372	6%	4,372	6%
2017	75,735	US	27,720	37%	China	6,679	9%	EU	3,819	5%	6,679	9%
2018	77,631	EU	17,925	23%	Japan	4,996	6%	US	4,320	6%	3,762	5%

Data Source: ASEAN Statistical Yearbooks.

also worry if rapidly depreciating assets like hydropower dams are transferred back into state ownership after the initial, most profitable operational period has passed. At the same time, foreign control of service provision in critical sectors can also generate vulnerabilities.

In SEA, Chinese investments related to service provision in two areas of *critical national infrastructure* stand out: electricity and telecommunications.[10] Chinese companies first entered the SEA electricity markets in a significant way with two major acquisitions in 2008. In Singapore, Huaneng bought Tuas Power—the smallest of three electricity-generating companies privatized by the government, supplying a quarter of the national market[11]—for US$3.04 billion, the largest-ever acquisition overseas by a Chinese power company at the time.[12] That same year, the State Grid Corporation of China bought a 40 per cent stake (US$1.58 billion) in the National Grid Corporation of the Philippines, with a twenty-five-year franchise to operate and manage the country's power transmission facilities. Domestic political opposition to the NGCP being "infected by a national security virus" and China controlling Manila's power supply caused the Benigno Aquino administration to suspend Chinese technical involvement in Grid operations in 2015.[13] Most recently—in March 2021 and therefore not covered in this report's dataset—the state-owned energy provider Electricité du Laos divested 90 per cent of its national transmission business to China Southern Power Grid to complete the much-delayed construction of Laos' national electricity grid for both domestic consumption and export to the region.[14]

Chinese investment has also picked up in the rapidly expanding and highly profitable telecommunications sector in SEA. Two large investments feature in our dataset: China Mobile's US$880 million acquisition of an 18 per cent stake in True Corp in Thailand in June 2014, a few weeks after the military coup when other foreign investments slumped; and China Telecom's US$860 million investment in Mislatel (shortly thereafter renamed Dito), set up in 2019 to break the longstanding telecommunications service duopoly in the Philippines. China Telecom holds a 40 per cent stake in Dito, the maximum allowed for a foreign company in the Philippines' telecom sector; while local partners Udenna and Chelsea Logistics hold 35 per cent and 25 per cent respectively in a deal reportedly worth US$5.4 billion overall.[15] The consortium has promised to bring highspeed internet to 84 per cent of the nation's population in five years.[16] These providers, like many others in SEA, use equipment from and collaborate in 5G development with Chinese firms, especially Huawei and ZTE. A recent survey found that Chinese firms are viewed as popular partners for building 5G infrastructure across SEA, and are most popular in Cambodia, Laos and Malaysia. Vietnam alone is unreceptive towards Huawei technology. Since mid-2020 though, many major SEA providers have tried to diversify away from Huawei, towards European firms Ericsson and Nokia.[17]

As is evident in the unfolding Huawei case, others' vulnerability could also arise from very large Chinese investments in *sectors or industries which are strategically important for China*. Two of the most obvious instances in our dataset relate to Beijing's quest for greater energy security. In 2009, state-owned PetroChina bought Singapore Petroleum Company for US$2.18 billion, gaining a foothold in Asia's largest oil trading centre and increasing its refining capacity just as the Chinese government introduced a market-based fuel pricing system and prices were expected to rise in China. By that point, PetroChina was already Asia's largest oil and gas producer, and the acquisition increased its flexibility in international oil pricing and trading. Strategically, acquiring such downstream fuel production complemented efforts by China's oil sector to buy upstream oil exploration assets around the world to secure energy supplies.[18] In 2014, privately owned Zhejiang Hengyi invested US$3.44 billion in 70 per cent stakes for a new oil refinery and petrochemical complex (Pulau Muara Besar) in oil-rich Brunei. In 2020, the consortium announced an additional investment of over US$13 billion into Phase II of the project, aiming to produce an additional 14 million tons of refined oil on top of the current production capacity of 8 million tons per year.[19]

In Myanmar in 2016, Zhuhai Zhenrong, one of the four licensed state importers of crude oil in China, won a contract to build an oil refinery in Dawei with a capacity of 8 million tons per year. At US$2.1 billion, this was the most valuable Chinese investment in Myanmar recorded in our dataset. This first large-scale refinery for Myanmar will refine oil imported from the Middle East, and from eventual domestic production from Myanmar's offshore oil blocks in the Andaman Sea. The refinery project was perceived to fit in China's Maritime Silk Road initiative and compete with Japanese and Thai investments in the Dawei Special Economic Zone.[20] Figure 8 maps these projects, as well as the other, more strategically significant Chinese energy investment in Myanmar, China National Petroleum Company's earlier (2009) US$1.02 billion investment to build pipelines further north on Myanmar's coast at Kyaukphyu. The gas pipeline carries natural gas from Myanmar's Shwe gas fields off Rakhine state in the west, cross-country and into Yunnan, the Chinese province bordering Myanmar. The parallel oil pipeline, which opened in 2015, is China's first overland access to shipments of crude oil from the Middle East, and thus a signature project to help mediate China's Malacca Straits dilemma. Its official carrying capacity is equivalent to the total capacity of Phases I and II of Pulau Muara Besar oil refineries in Brunei.[21] Our calculations using 2017–20 figures suggest that, at full capacity, the Kyaukphyu gas pipeline could carry between 8.5 per cent and 12.7 per cent of China's annual gas imports, while the oil pipeline could carry between 4.1 per cent and 5.5 per cent of its yearly oil imports.[22]

1.3.2 Strategic Integration

SEA countries hosting investments of strategic significance for China undergo varying degrees of integration into Chinese strategic arenas and interests. On the lighter end of the spectrum are companies and services such as Singapore Petroleum Company, which give China's SOEs stakes in the key nodes and clearing houses of the international oil markets. Further along the

Figure 8: Map of Dawei Refinery, Special Economic Zones, and Kyaukphyu Pipelines in Myanmar

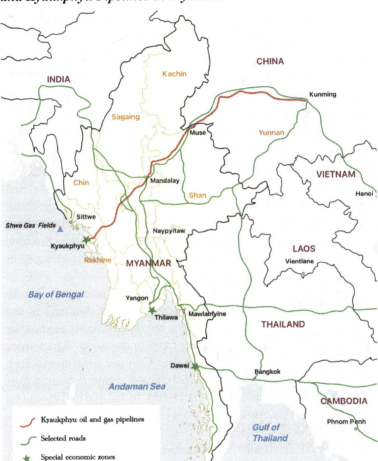

Data Source: China Global Investment Tracker 2019 Fall Dataset (accessed in January 2020), China Global Investment Tracker 2021 Spring Dataset (accessed in August 2021) and ASEAN Statistical Yearbooks.

spectrum are countries that host assets such as oil refineries, which may not be owned outright by Chinese firms but were developed with Chinese investment to provide crucial diversification for China's energy supplies. Most integrated with China's strategic interests are those countries with critical Chinese infrastructure on their territories, including pipelines but also the deep-sea ports which usually accompany pipelines and refineries and provide *strategic access to sea routes*. Myanmar provides an excellent example—Chinese investments in the energy projects at Dawei and Kyaukphyu entail building port facilities where large oil tankers can dock and potentially creating conditions for hosting other deep-sea vessels accessing the Bay of Bengal and Indian Ocean.[23] Myanmar's strategic integration dilemma is encapsulated in China now having concrete stakes in its domestic political stability, including the management of ethnic insurgencies both on their shared border in eastern Myanmar as well as in Rakhine state in west Myanmar where all this infrastructure is being built (see Figure 8).

Other strategically located port projects that have seen Chinese investments might give access to key maritime domains in the South China Sea and Malacca Straits, but to date, many are neither large enough nor have they yet proven sustainable. Apart from Pulau Muara Besar in Brunei, smaller Chinese investments (not recorded in our dataset due to size) helped create container port facilities in Kuala Tanjung in Sumatra, Indonesia, and in Kuantan on the east coast of peninsular Malaysia (both in 2018). Both projects have strong local commercial dynamics and are associated with major special economic zones/industrial parks in collaboration with Chinese investors and listed among the official BRI projects. On the west coast of the Malay peninsula, the recently cancelled Melaka deep-sea port would have given Chinese investors stakes in an important new facility on the Malacca Straits.

Various *transport infrastructure* projects are also meant to help mainland SEA integrate physically with southwestern China. However, these mainly rail projects have been slow to take off, partly due to logjams created by two changes of government in

Thailand since the plan was first agreed to in 2008. Thailand contains the crucial transitional segment of the planned north-south line from Kunming to Bangkok, to link up with existing railways running south. The bulk of Chinese investments realized to date centres on building the rail link northwards connecting Vientiane-Boten-Kunming. The Thai section linking Bangkok to Nong Khai at the Thai-Lao border has been mired by disagreement over design, financing technical assistance. The Thai government is self-financing the building and has announced it would be issuing contracts only for the first part of the link from Bangkok to Nakhon Ratchasima.[24] As of November 2022, only 15 per cent of this first part had been constructed.[25] Other large Chinese investments in SEA transport connectivity mostly promote domestic road and rail links—in our dataset every SEA country, except for Myanmar, recorded such investments.

1.4 Conclusion

Over the 2005–19 period, Chinese investments in SEA grew significantly. While China is not yet a dominant investor in the region, we can expect its significance to grow, especially given the broad scope and domain of its large investments in SEA. This report presents a detailed country-by-country analysis of the patterns of large Chinese investments in the key sectors. As this overview outlines, Chinese investments play increasingly important roles for every SEA country, but the variations in distribution and in political and strategic significance suggest that China's importance and influence can take quite different forms. Thus far, Chinese investments create the most obvious vulnerabilities in the three mainland countries—Cambodia, Laos and Myanmar. But the developing patterns of dependence and vulnerability are dynamic and hard to predict in many of the other SEA countries because of fairly specific reasons for their relative exposure to Chinese investments to date. Certainly, countries like Myanmar, Brunei—and to a lesser extent—Indonesia and Malaysia, which host Chinese-funded strategic infrastructure projects, may be taking risks. So far, however, we have no instances with which to assess their prospects of being held hostage on the basis of these exposures. Others—like the Philippines and pre-2018 Malaysia— have overall low levels of, or dependency on, Chinese investment, but a handful of large investments with strategic significance.

In sum, this Overview and Analysis section and the detailed Quantitative Report create a baseline for comparing Chinese investment across SEA, and provides the wider context of large, multi-sectoral Chinese investments in the region to facilitate informed analysis of the significance of specific sectors or projects. It also provides a basis for further political analysis to help explain the variation in levels, patterns, and effects of large Chinese investments across SEA countries and sectors.

1.5 Epilogue: The COVID Years and Beyond

This study provides data and analysis for the years between 2005 and 2019 only. The World Health Organization declared COVID-19 a pandemic on 11 March 2020. At the time of preparation for publication, we were able to access some data to extend parts of our dataset up to the first half of 2022 only. The COVID-19 pandemic, as a rare and extreme event, will clearly have impacted and continue to affect Chinese investments, including in SEA countries. However, as of 2023, we do not yet have sufficient data to conduct a robust assessment of the nature and extent of these impacts. Our analysis of the 2005–19 data presented here captures the trends and patterns of Chinese investments in SEA countries *prior* to the COVID-19 pandemic, and will act as a baseline to help understand key changes in patterns of Chinese investments in SEA during and after the pandemic. As more multi-year investment data post-2019 become available in the coming years, we shall be in a better position to extend the timeframe of our study and to assess the demonstrated impacts of the COVID-19 pandemic on the longer-term patterns of Chinese investments in SEA countries.[26]

Meanwhile, it is evident that the disruptions caused by the pandemic led to declines in overall Chinese investment overseas, as well as delays in many ongoing and planned projects and delivery. The economic slowdown engendered by COVID lockdowns and restrictions hit China in early 2020 before spreading to the rest of the world, significantly reducing economic activity and productivity. The Chinese economy has required more resources and stimulus from its own financial institutions to recover from strict zero-COVID policies and the bursting of the real estate bubble. The political situation in China, including the significant consolidation of President Xi Jinping's power, and the centre's efforts to rein in large companies and redistribute wealth redistribution also placed constraints on outward investment flows. At the same time, potential returns from overseas investments seemed increasingly problematic with COVID impacts coming on top of debt defaults in multiple BRI countries ranging from Laos to Zimbabwe.[27] Many recipients of foreign investment and loans also became more focused on fighting COVID-induced economic hardship than pushing projects requiring large foreign investments.

Various contemporaneous surveys concur that Chinese overseas investments declined between 2019 and 2021.[28] Herrero (2022) uses CGIT and Mergermarket data to show that China's overall outbound FDI had dropped 72 per cent by 2020–21 from the average reached during 2015–19.[29] Moreover, a large number of BRI projects around the world faced financial and operational difficulties and had to be delayed or abandoned.[30] Within Southeast Asia, Wang (2022) found that about 20 per cent of BRI projects were "seriously affected" by COVID measure as of June 2020, with another 30–40 per cent being "somewhat affected".[31]

Yet, Southeast Asia grew in significance (relative to other parts of the world) in the Chinese overseas investment landscape. Southeast Asia became the top BRI investment destination in 2020, even as overall Chinese outward investments declined. Wang (2022) notes that by the end of 2021, parts of China's BRI investments saw a year-on-year growth rate of 14 per cent, with seven Southeast Asian countries ranking among the top ten recipients (Singapore, Indonesia, Malaysia, Vietnam, Laos, Thailand, and Cambodia). Notably, Indonesia was hosting the largest number of BRI projects (forty) in the region across a variety of sectors, followed by Cambodia with seventeen and Laos twelve. Various high-profile Chinese-funded infrastructure projects including the Jakarta-Bandung high-speed railway continued apace throughout the pandemic, and the China-Laos Railway project was even officially opened at the end of 2021.

Apart from the pandemic, Chinese investment in Southeast Asia were negatively affected by other significant developments since 2019. One specific impact was the 2021 coup in Myanmar, which has created delays and uncertainty over large Chinese investments in the deep seaport at the Kyaukphyu SEZ, the Muse-Mandalay electric railway, and the New Yangon City project.[32]

At a broader regional level, the economic strains created by the pandemic have led to a new direction in ASEAN's regional connectivity strategy. This plan now stresses maximizing the potential of intra-ASEAN economic integration and explicitly links the development of its infrastructure connectivity with promoting more resilient regional supply chains. Thus, to withstand future shocks, ASEAN can be expected to invest in different connectivity plans as alternatives to the many China-centric regional supply chains.[33] This should be read as a push for more diverse sources of investments, markets, and value chains, not a reduced emphasis on Chinese investment *per se*. Thus, the aim is to court new sources of investment and to increase volumes of investment from other existing sources, rather than to diminish the amount of Chinese investment.[34]

From the Chinese side, we can expect continued attention to investment in Southeast Asia, probably with accentuated strategic rationale as China grapples with post-COVID recovery and positioning itself in a more fractious geopolitical contest. Southeast Asia is likely to play an important role in President Xi's Global Development Initiative, announced in 2021, and his Global Security and Global Civilization initiatives launched in 2022. Beijing suddenly announced the lifting of China's draconian domestic COVID control measures at the end of 2022, and the relaxation of international travel restrictions from January 2023. The effects of these policy reversals upon outbound investment and fulfilment continue to unfold.

Section 2
QUANTITATIVE REPORT

2.1 Overview of Chinese Investments[35] in Southeast Asia, 2005–19

Absolute Scale

Overall, foreign investments in SEA originating from China exhibited a general upward trend between 2005[36] and 2019,[37] rising approximately twentyfold during this fifteen-year period. This trend is evident across different datasets that use differing measures of foreign investments (see Figure 9). Foreign direct investment is a commonly used measure of cross-border investments that captures foreign acquisition—by both state-owned entities and private entities—of ownership of target enterprises in destination countries.[38] Data from ASEAN's Statistical Yearbooks show that Chinese FDI to SEA grew exponentially from just over US$500 million in 2005 to roughly US$10 billion in 2018, peaking at US$13.7 billion in 2017. A broader measure of foreign investments would take into account cross-border transactions that involve not only ownership acquisition but also service provision. The CGIT database adopts this broader measure of foreign investments to track "large" Chinese overseas investments (those that are worth at least US$100 million). According to the CGIT database, Chinese investments in SEA soared from US$1.3 billion in 2005 to nearly US$31 billion in 2019, peaking at US$33.5 billion in 2018. A closer look at the trend of Chinese investments in SEA reveals that Chinese investments in SEA experienced its first phase of rapid expansion between 2009 and 2011, right after the end of the global financial crisis, and a second phase of rapid increase between 2014 and 2017, following the official announcement of Beijing's BRI. Indeed, the vast majority of very large (at least US$1 billion)

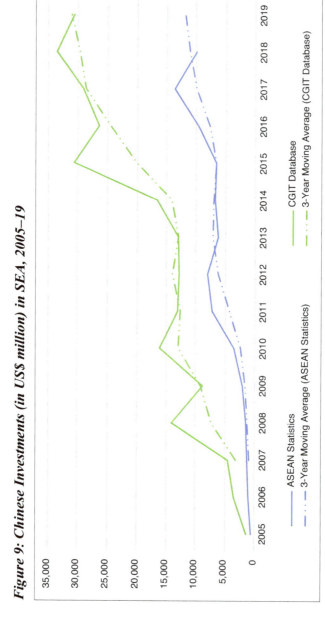

Figure 9: Chinese Investments (in US$ million) in SEA, 2005–19

Data Source: China Global Investment Tracker 2019 Fall Dataset (accessed in January 2020), China Global Investment Tracker 2021 Spring Dataset (accessed in August 2021) and ASEAN Statistical Yearbooks.

Chinese investments came after the advent of the BRI in 2013 for all SEA countries except Vietnam and Myanmar (as indicated in red and pink on Figure 10). However, between 2018 and the time of writing (late 2021), this growth appears to be slowing down or even declining modestly.

Relative Importance
Despite the substantial surge in the absolute amounts of Chinese investments in SEA between 2005 and 2019, the relative importance of Chinese FDI[39]—as compared to other sources of FDI in SEA—did not increase as significantly. While China's share of total FDI in SEA more than doubled—from an average of 3 per cent in 2005–10 to an average of 7 per cent in 2011–18—China had yet to establish itself as a dominant foreign investor in SEA. Table 1 displays annual FDI flows into ASEAN from 2005 to 2018. Only in 2012 and 2018 was China among the top three non-ASEAN foreign investors in SEA; in these two years, it lagged behind the US and Japan, and the EU and Japan, respectively. Even when China was the third largest non-ASEAN foreign investor in SEA, China's share of ASEAN's total annual FDI (at 7 per cent in both 2012 and 2018) was only half that of the second largest investor, Japan (which accounted for 13 per cent in 2012 and 14 per cent in 2018). During 2005–18, the EU remained as the largest non-ASEAN foreign investor in SEA; its total FDI amount approximated US$235 billion, which was roughly three times as large as China's (at US$77.8 billion). Following the EU were Japan and the US, whose absolute amounts of FDI in SEA between 2005 and 2018 totalled roughly US$174 billion and US$173 billion, respectively.

Distribution
In addition to the general trend of absolute increase in quantity, diversification in distribution was another prominent feature of Chinese investments in SEA between 2005 and 2019. During this period, China diversified its investments in SEA not only across industrial sectors but also across SEA host countries. As displayed

Figure 10: Number of Chinese Investments Worth at Least US$1 billion in SEA Countries, 2005–19

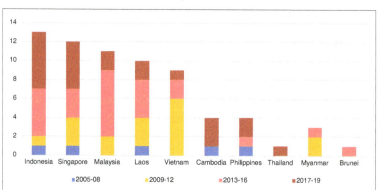

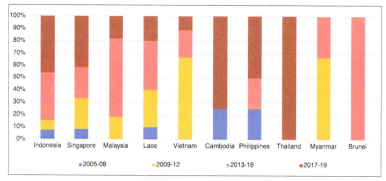

Data Source: China Global Investment Tracker 2019 Fall Dataset (accessed in January 2020), China Global Investment Tracker 2021 Spring Dataset (accessed in August 2021).

in Figure 11, Chinese investments in SEA were overwhelmingly in the *energy* sector between 2005 and 2010. On average, the energy sector accounted for over 70 per cent of Chinese investments in SEA during this period, peaking at 100 per cent in 2007. But from 2011 onwards, China started to diversify its investments in SEA across various industrial sectors. For example, in 2012, metals were the industrial sector that received the largest amount of Chinese investments in SEA among the four sectors being

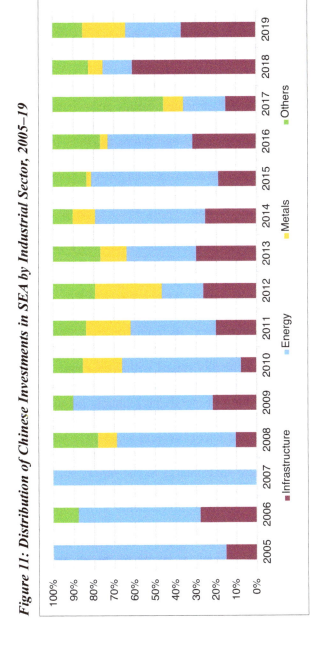

Figure 11: Distribution of Chinese Investments in SEA by Industrial Sector, 2005–19

Data Source: China Global Investment Tracker 2019 Fall Dataset (accessed in January 2020), China Global Investment Tracker 2021 Spring Dataset (accessed in August 2021).

compared (infrastructure, energy, metals and others[40]). The metals sector accounted for 32 per cent of total Chinese investments in SEA in that year, followed by the infrastructure sector, at 26 per cent. In 2018 and 2019, infrastructure was the sector that received the largest proportion, accounting for 61 per cent and 37 per cent of total Chinese investments in SEA, respectively. Overall, the average shares of the infrastructure, metals and others sectors in 2011–19 more than doubled to 30 per cent, 14 per cent and 22 per cent respectively from their average shares in 2005–10, whereas that of the energy sector halved to 35 per cent in 2011–19.

In terms of amounts invested in each SEA industrial sector, Chinese investments in *infrastructure* grew substantially between 2005 and 2018, multiplying from US$200 million in 2005 to US$20 billion in 2018 (even though the amount nearly halved in 2019, to US$11 billion) (see Figure 12). By contrast, Chinese *energy* investments exhibited wide fluctuations during the same period. Having fluctuated mainly below US$8 billion prior to 2014, Chinese energy investments in SEA surged to a peak of US$19 billion in 2015 before dropping back to around US$8 billion in recent years. By comparison, Chinese *metals* investments in SEA did not display patterns of dramatic changes; the annual amounts generally stayed within the range of US$1.5 billion to US$4 billion between 2008 and 2018, with a record high of nearly US$6.5 billion in metals investments logged in 2019. While significant changes in the trends of Chinese investments in the infrastructure and energy sectors since 2014 were usually associated with several SEA host countries, dramatic changes in the pattern of Chinese investments in the *others* sector in SEA from 2014 onwards were attributed largely to Singapore. For example, the peak of Chinese investments in the *others* sector in 2017 (at nearly US$16 billion) pertained to Chinese investors acquiring ownership in the logistics, consumer and property industries in Singapore, with a combined investment value of more than US$12 billion.

In terms of the distribution of Chinese investments across SEA host countries, a turning point was reached in 2008 (see Figure 13).

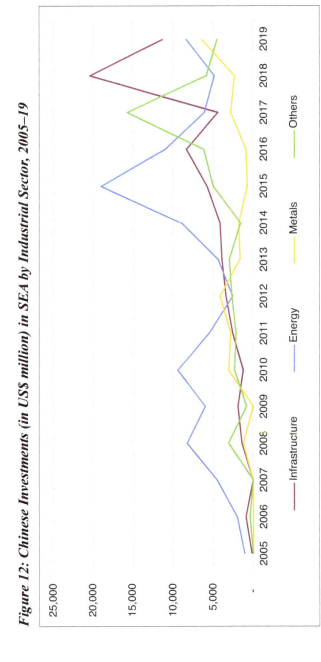

Figure 12: Chinese Investments (in US$ million) in SEA by Industrial Sector, 2005–19

Data Source: China Global Investment Tracker 2019 Fall Dataset (accessed in January 2020), China Global Investment Tracker 2021 Spring Dataset (accessed in August 2021).

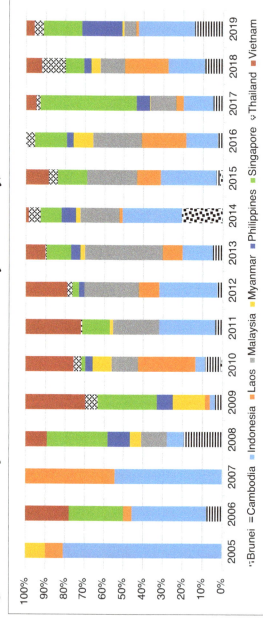

Figure 13: Distribution of Chinese Investments in SEA by Host Country, 2005–19

Data Source: China Global Investment Tracker 2019 Fall Dataset (accessed in January 2020), China Global Investment Tracker 2021 Spring Dataset (accessed in August 2021).

Between 2005 and 2007, China invested in barely half of the ten SEA countries[41] at most, and its investments were concentrated significantly in Indonesia. For example, Indonesia made up approximately 80 per cent of total Chinese investments in SEA in 2005. From 2008 onwards, China began to spread its investments in SEA across a larger number of host countries. Every year, at least seven out of the ten countries in SEA received Chinese investments. Among the new host countries was Malaysia, which became one of the top three recipients of Chinese investments in SEA in 2008 and retained this position between 2010 and 2017. Indonesia, while remaining an important destination of Chinese investments in SEA, declined in relative importance, with its share of total Chinese investments in SEA shrinking from an average of nearly 60 per cent in 2005–7, to an average of approximately 20 per cent in 2008–19. Indonesia, Singapore and Malaysia were the top three destinations in 2008–19, accounting for 20 per cent, 19 per cent and 18 per cent respectively of total Chinese investments in SEA during this twelve-year period.[42]

2.2 Chinese Investments in Specific SEA Countries, 2005–19

During 2005–19, Indonesia, Singapore and Malaysia were the top three host countries of Chinese investments in SEA (CGIT data), together accounting for nearly 60 per cent of total Chinese investments in SEA during this fifteen-year period (see Table 7). Singapore, Cambodia and Myanmar were more attractive destinations for Chinese investments involving ownership acquisition than the other SEA countries.

Indonesia

Absolute Scale
Overall, Chinese investments in Indonesia increased significantly during 2005–19. According to the CGIT database, Indonesia was the largest recipient of Chinese investments in SEA in

Table 7: Chinese Investments (in US$ million) in SEA by Host Country, 2005–19

Ownership Acquisition and Service Provision			Ownership Acquisition only		
SEA Country	Amount	Share	SEA Country	Amount	Share
Indonesia	53,720	21%	Singapore	35,840	28%
Singapore	46,310	18%	Indonesia	25,530	20%
Malaysia	43,060	17%	Malaysia	18,720	15%
Laos	28,650	11%	Laos	11,960	9%
Vietnam	25,500	10%	Cambodia	9,470	7%
Cambodia	16,240	6%	Philippines	6,830	5%
Philippines	15,290	6%	Myanmar	6,420	5%
Thailand	11,550	5%	Vietnam	5,740	4%
Myanmar	9,600	4%	Thailand	5,090	4%
Brunei	4,110	2%	Brunei	3,440	3%
Total	*254,030*		*Total*	*129,040*	

Data Source: China Global Investment Tracker 2019 Fall Dataset (accessed in January 2020), China Global Investment Tracker 2021 Spring Dataset (accessed in August 2021).

2005–19, accounting for 21 per cent of total Chinese investments in SEA during this fifteen-year period. Starting at slightly over US$1 billion in 2005, the absolute level of Chinese investments in Indonesia multiplied more than eightfold to US$8.7 billion in 2019, with wide fluctuations in 2007–11 and 2013–16 (see Figure 14[43]). Specifically, during the global financial crisis, Chinese investments in Indonesia plunged from nearly US$2.5 billion in 2007 to a mere US$230 million in 2009, but it quickly bounced back to above the pre-crisis level in 2011, at US$3.7 billion. It is worth noting that the drastic decline in Chinese investments in Indonesia during 2007–9 was due primarily to a substantial reduction in cross-border transactions involving service provision (where Chinese entities mainly served as contractors to undertake such activities as installation and maintenance of equipment, technical evaluation, and supervision of the construction process), whereas the post-crisis recovery resulted largely from a notable increase in Chinese acquisition of asset ownership in Indonesia. After the official launch of Beijing's BRI, Chinese investments in Indonesia more than quadrupled from roughly US$2 billion in 2013 to US$8.5 billion in 2015—the second-highest level between 2005 and 2019. In 2015, Chinese investments in Indonesia accounted for 28 per cent of total Chinese investments in SEA in that year—the highest share among all SEA countries. The substantial amount of Chinese investments in Indonesia in 2015 was attributed primarily to Chinese investments in two coal-fired power plants and one hydropower plant in Indonesia, whose investment value totalled US$4.19 billion. However, Chinese investments in Indonesia halved to US$4.3 billion in 2016, which was a major contributor to the overall decrease in Chinese investments in SEA during 2015–16. Yet, the investment amount recovered again in 2017–19, reaching a record high of US$8.7 billion in 2019. In general, annual Chinese investments in Indonesia since the official announcement of Beijing's BRI in 2013 eclipsed those in the pre-BRI period, with the 2013–19 average (at US$5.6 billion) being roughly three times as large as the 2005–12 average (at US$1.8 billion).

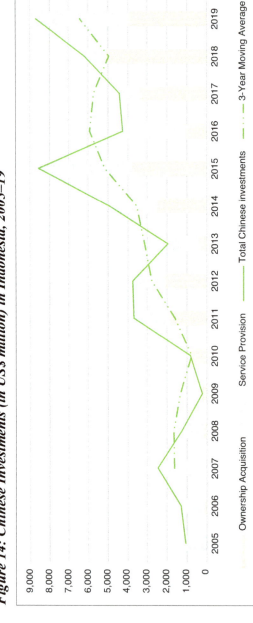

Figure 14: Chinese Investments (in US$ million) in Indonesia, 2005–19

Data Source: China Global Investment Tracker 2019 Fall Dataset (accessed in January 2020), China Global Investment Tracker 2021 Spring Dataset (accessed in August 2021).

Relative Importance
Chinese FDI grew in importance for Indonesia after the global
financial crisis and more notably, after the BRI was launched.
During 2005–8, China did not feature among the top three non-
ASEAN foreign investors in Indonesia, which tended to be Japan,
the EU and US. During these four years, China's share of total FDI
in Indonesia lagged considerably behind that of the third largest
investor, with the largest difference being 15 percentage points.
From 2009 to 2013, while China still hardly featured among the
top three non-ASEAN foreign investors, the gap between China's
share of total FDI in Indonesia and that of the third largest investor
narrowed significantly, to no more than 3 percentage points. But
this shrinking difference was more a result of decreases in the
share of the third largest foreign investor in Indonesia than of
increases in China's share, as Indonesia saw stagnant or declining
FDI from traditional foreign investors, especially the US and EU
(see Table 8). By 2014–18, China was among the top three non-
ASEAN foreign investors in Indonesia in each year; its share
of total FDI reached double digits in 2017–18 for the first time
since 2005. Nevertheless, Chinese FDI still lagged behind: during
2005–18, Japan remained the largest source, providing 27 per cent
of Indonesia's total FDI compared to China's 5 per cent.

Distribution
As the volume of Chinese investments in Indonesia began to
recover shortly after the global financial crisis, China also
started to diversify its investments in Indonesia across industrial
sectors. During 2005–10, Chinese investments in Indonesia
were predominantly in the energy sector, which accounted
for an average share of 97 per cent during this six-year period
(see Figure 15). From 2011 onwards, China began to invest in
Indonesia's infrastructure and metals sectors. China's annual
investments in Indonesia's infrastructure sector more than doubled
from US$1.1 billion in 2011 to US$2.5 billion in 2019, with the
most noticeable increase observed between 2017 and 2018 (from
US$1.3 billion to US$2.9 billion). Infrastructure's average share of

Table 8: Top Three (Non-ASEAN) Foreign Investors in Indonesia, 2005–18

Year	Total	Largest Investor			Second Largest Investor			Third Largest Investor			Chinese FDI to Indonesia (in US$ million)	
		Investor	Amount	Share	Investor	Amount	Share	Investor	Amount	Share	Amount	Share
2005	8,336	US	3,440	41%	EU	1,543	19%	Japan	1,542	19%	300	4%
2006	4,914	EU	1,995	41%	Japan	1,057	22%	Australia	366	7%	124	3%
2007	6,928	EU	2,409	35%	Japan	1,125	16%	US	1,093	16%	117	2%
2008	8,340	Japan	1,518	18%	EU	1,063	13%	US	873	10%	380	5%
2009	4,877	Japan	896	18%	China	359	7%	EU	299	6%	359	7%
2010	13,770	Japan	3,730	27%	Australia	894	6%	US	572	4%	354	3%
2011	19,242	Japan	6,175	32%	EU	2,994	16%	S. Korea	725	4%	215	1%
2012	19,138	Japan	7,962	42%	US	830	4%	S. Korea	692	4%	335	2%
2013	18,444	Japan	5,557	30%	US	1,064	6%	S. Korea	981	5%	591	3%
2014	21,810	Japan	5,793	27%	China	1,068	5%	S. Korea	953	4%	1,068	5%
2015	16,642	Japan	4,010	24%	US	603	4%	China	324	2%	324	2%
2016	3,921	Japan	2,499	64%	EU	1,554	40%	China	355	9%	355	9%
2017	20,579	EU	5,349	26%	Japan	3,913	19%	China	1,994	10%	1,994	10%
2018	21,980	Japan	4,937	22%	China	2,143	10%	US	1,067	5%	2,143	10%

Data Source: ASEAN Statistical Yearbooks.

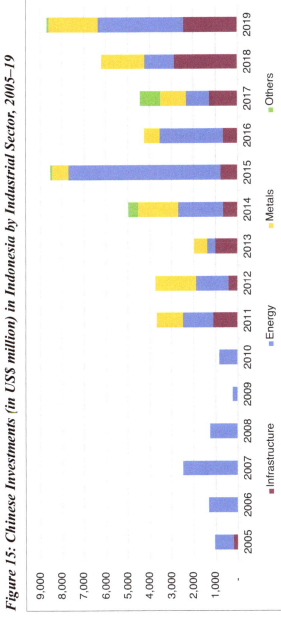

Figure 15: Chinese Investments (in US$ million) in Indonesia by Industrial Sector, 2005–19

Data Source: China Global Investment Tracker 2019 Fall Dataset (accessed in January 2020), China Global Investment Tracker 2021 Spring Dataset (accessed in August 2021).

total Chinese investments in Indonesia rose from a mere 3 per cent in 2005–10, to 26 per cent during 2011–19. Meanwhile, China's annual investments in Indonesia's metals sector fluctuated around US$1.4 billion during 2011–19, and their average share grew from nil in 2005–10 to nearly 30 per cent in 2011–19. In contrast, the average share of China's energy investments in Indonesia during 2011–19 plummeted to 42 per cent (less than half of their average share during 2005–10), although the amount of China's annual investments in Indonesia's energy sector was generally higher in 2011–19 (averaging US$2.4 billion) than in 2005–10 (averaging US$1.2 billion).

Overall, Indonesia's *energy* sector received US$28.3 billion in Chinese investments during 2005–19, constituting 53 per cent of total Chinese investments in Indonesia during this fifteen-year period. Indeed, on average, Indonesia saw the largest share (one-third) of Chinese energy investments in SEA, which even exceeded 50 per cent in 2005–7 and 2012. The hydropower industry accounted for roughly a quarter of China's total energy investments in Indonesia, with the vast majority of hydro-related investments (at US$7.8 billion) made from 2015 onwards. Among the most valuable contracts were a US$1.71 billion contract for the first phase of the Kayan I Hydropower Plant Project signed by China Railway Construction in 2015, and a US$1.36 billion contract for part of the Kayan River Cascade Hydropower Project signed by Power Construction Corp in 2019. These Kayan projects together accounted for almost 40 per cent of total Chinese hydropower investments in Indonesia during 2005–19.

Nearly 60 per cent of China's total energy investments in Indonesia were in the coal industry. While most Chinese coal-related investments in Indonesia were construction contracts, the average value of construction contracts (at US$476 million) was lower than the average value of transactions that involved Chinese acquisition of ownership in Indonesian coal-fired power plants or coal companies (at US$670 million). While Chinese coal-related construction contracts were carried out throughout 2005–19, Chinese acquisitions of coal-related ownership were predominantly in the 2010s. For example, in 2015, Shenhua Group and China National Machinery Industry Corporation invested US$1.32 billion (through ownership acquisition) and US$1.16 billion (through construction contract) respectively to build coal-fired power plants in Banten—together accounting for nearly 30 per cent of total Chinese investments in Indonesia that year. In 2016, Harbin Electric Company Limited invested US$1.47 billion (through construction contract) to build a new clean coal power station in Tanjung Jati, also in West Java—the single largest Chinese investment in the coal industry in Indonesia to date.

By comparison, Chinese investments in Indonesia's *infrastructure* sector totalled US$11.5 billion (21 per cent of total Chinese investments in the country). Notably, Chinese investments in the Jakarta-Bandung high-speed railway project in 2018 accounted for roughly one fifth of Chinese infrastructure investments in Indonesia during 2005–19. This US$2.46 billion high-speed railway project was the third most valuable Chinese infrastructure investment project in SEA in a single year, following the Laos-China railway project in 2018 (valued at US$4.17 billion) and the Thailand-China railway project in 2018 (valued at US$2.69 billion). Across SEA, Indonesia accounted for 16 per cent of total Chinese infrastructure investments in SEA during 2005–19, slightly after Malaysia (at 21 per cent) and Singapore (at 17 per cent).

Slightly ahead of the infrastructure sector, the *metals* sector received US$12.4 billion in Chinese investments, which accounted for 23 per cent of total Chinese investments in Indonesia. Indonesia's share of Chinese metals investments in SEA averaged nearly 50 per cent between 2008 and 2019—the highest average share among all SEA countries—and notably, all Chinese metals investments in SEA went to Indonesia in 2014 and 2015. Around 70 per cent of all Chinese metals investments in Indonesia went to the steel industry. In particular, China Nickel Resources Holdings Co. Ltd invested US$1.26 billion in 2012 to build PT Batulicin Steel in South Kalimantan. This steel plant, in which China would have 61 per cent ownership, was expected to have an annual processing capacity of 1 million tonnes of iron bar and 0.6 million tonnes of ferronickel. Another significant Chinese metals investment was the US$1.16 billion Huayue Nickel Project in Sulawesi in 2019. This investment, made by a Chinese consortium consisting of Zhejiang Huayou Cobalt, China Molybdenum and Tsingshan Holding Group, came at a time when the Jokowi government decided to ban raw nickel ore exports from 2020 to stimulate the domestic processing industry.

Singapore

Absolute Scale

Overall, Singapore accounted for 18 per cent of total Chinese investments in SEA during 2005–19 according to the CGIT dataset, making Singapore the second largest recipient of Chinese investments in SEA. Chinese investments in Singapore gradually increased since 2010 and remained relatively stable from 2015 onwards (except the peak in 2017). Following the global financial crisis, these plunged from US$4.4 billion in 2008 to only US$320 million in 2010 (see Figure 16). However, it recovered gradually afterwards, rising to above the pre-crisis level in 2015. Between 2015 and 2019, annual Chinese investments fluctuated around US$4 billion, except in 2017 when it topped US$14 billion. That record high was primarily due to a Chinese consortium (Hopu Investment Management, Hillhouse Capital Group, Vanke Group and Bank of China Group Investment) acquiring Singapore-listed Global Logistic Properties, the largest warehouse operator in Asia. The acquisition, valued at US$9 billion, accounted for nearly two-thirds of Chinese investments in Singapore in 2017. Chinese acquisition of asset ownership constituted a significant share (usually more than 70 per cent) of Chinese investments in Singapore throughout 2005–19, whereas cross-border transactions involving service provision were much more limited. This split of Chinese investment types is closely related to the industrial sectors in Singapore that Chinese investments were most interested in, as discussed in the *Distribution* section below.

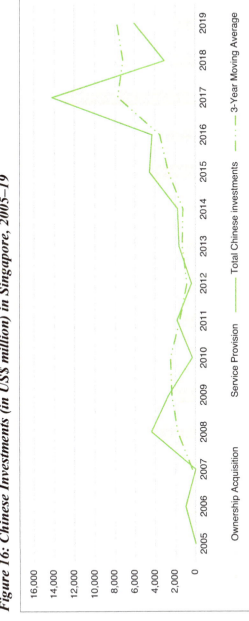

Figure 16: Chinese Investments (in US$ million) in Singapore, 2005–19

Data Source: China Global Investment Tracker 2019 Fall Dataset (accessed in January 2020), China Global Investment Tracker 2021 Spring Dataset (accessed in August 2021).

Relative Importance
Overall, China could be considered the third most important source of FDI in Singapore during 2005–18, after the EU and US. As Table 9 shows, China was the third largest non-ASEAN foreign investor in Singapore between 2008 and 2016 (except in 2010 and 2013) and the second largest investor in 2017 (due to the acquisition of Global Logistic Properties mentioned above). In addition, China's share of total FDI in Singapore grew in significance from 2011, with an average share of 8 per cent in 2011–18, four times higher than its average share in 2005–10. Nevertheless, China was still not as important a foreign investor in Singapore as were the EU and US. During 2005–18, the EU was the largest non-ASEAN foreign investor in Singapore for the most part, accounting for approximately 25 per cent of total FDI in Singapore during this fourteen-year period. The US was usually the second largest foreign investor in Singapore, providing nearly 20 per cent of total FDI between 2005 and 2018. In contrast, China only accounted for 6 per cent of total FDI in Singapore during the same period. During 2005–18, China invested a total of US$40.4 billion, which was less than a quarter of the total FDI from the EU (US$165.7 billion) and less than a third of the total FDI from the US (at US$130.5 billion).

Distribution
As shown in Figure 17, Chinese investments in Singapore shifted significantly from the energy and infrastructure sectors to the *others* sector from 2011. Large Chinese investments in the *energy* sector took the form of acquisitions of Tuas Power in 2008 (at a value of US$3.04 billion) and Singapore Petroleum Company in 2009 (at a value of US$2.18 billion). These accounted for approximately 70 per cent and 80 per cent of total Chinese investments in Singapore in 2008 and 2009 respectively, but thereafter the energy sector's share fell and accounted for no more than 5 per cent in 2017 and 2019. Similarly, the *infrastructure* sector showed sporadic large spikes, accounting for 100 per cent of total Chinese investments in Singapore in 2006, 2010 and 2012,

Table 9: Top Three (Non-ASEAN) Foreign Investors in Singapore, 2005–18

Year	Total	Largest Investor			Second Largest Investor			Third Largest Investor			Chinese FDI to Singapore (in US$ million)	
		Investor	Amount	Share	Investor	Amount	Share	Investor	Amount	Share	Amount	Share
2005	14,373	EU	6,072	42%	Japan	1,800	13%	India	379	3%	69	0%
2006	27,681	EU	5,316	19%	Japan	3,312	12%	US	1,926	7%	617	2%
2007	31,550	EU	11,503	36%	US	2,949	9%	Japan	1,408	4%	594	2%
2008	22,802	EU	8,463	37%	Japan	1,493	7%	China	478	2%	478	2%
2009	18,917	US	3,306	17%	EU	1,336	7%	China	1,049	6%	1,049	6%
2010	57,214	EU	16,929	30%	US	6,915	12%	India	3,643	6%	699	1%
2011	39,887	EU	15,991	40%	US	6,465	16%	China	5,467	14%	5,467	14%
2012	60,102	US	13,784	23%	India	6,982	12%	China	5,970	10%	5,970	10%
2013	56,671	EU	14,313	25%	US	9,923	18%	Japan	2,662	5%	2,508	4%
2014	73,285	EU	23,878	33%	US	18,287	25%	China	4,168	6%	4,168	6%
2015	59,702	US	17,784	30%	EU	15,266	26%	China	3,991	7%	3,991	7%
2016	73,864	EU	32,336	44%	US	18,941	26%	China	4,372	6%	4,372	6%
2017	75,735	US	27,720	37%	China	6,679	9%	EU	3,819	5%	6,679	9%
2018	77,631	EU	17,925	23%	Japan	4,996	6%	US	4,320	6%	3,762	5%

Data Source: ASEAN Statistical Yearbooks.

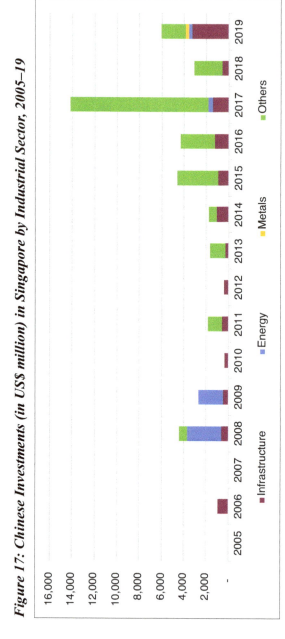

Figure 17: Chinese Investments (in US$ million) in Singapore by Industrial Sector, 2005–19

Data Source: China Global Investment Tracker 2019 Fall Dataset (accessed in January 2020), China Global Investment Tracker 2021 Spring Dataset (accessed in August 2021).

but the sector's average share between 2013 and 2019 only stood at 30 per cent. One of the most significant Chinese infrastructure investments in Singapore was the acquisition of Singapore Aircraft Leasing Enterprise by the Bank of China in 2006, at a price of US$970 million. In 2010 and 2017, Singapore had the largest share of total Chinese infrastructure investments in SEA among the ten SEA countries, accounting for 26 per cent and 33 per cent, respectively. By comparison, the *others* sector, which accounted for less than 5 per cent of total Chinese investments in Singapore prior to 2011, had an average share of 61 per cent between 2011 and 2019. Within this sector, logistics received the largest amount. As mentioned previously, in 2017, a Chinese consortium acquired Singapore-listed Global Logistics Properties for US$9 billion. In the same year, Chinese conglomerate HNA Group invested US$1 billion in Singaporean logistics firm CWT Ltd. Apart from the logistics subsector, the consumer subsector also received sizeable amounts of Chinese investments. In particular, Alibaba, a Chinese technology company specializing in e-commerce, acquired Lazada, a Singaporean e-commerce company, for US$1 billion in 2016 and invested another US$3 billion in Lazada in 2017–18. Overall, the others sector accounted for 60 per cent of total Chinese investments in Singapore between 2005 and 2019, followed by the infrastructure sector (26 per cent), energy sector (13 per cent) and metals sector (1 per cent) respectively. When the absolute amounts of Chinese investments received by the four industrial sectors are compared, the others sector received a total of US$27.9 billion during 2005–19, whereas the infrastructure and energy sectors received US$12.2 billion and US$5.9 billion, respectively.

Malaysia

Absolute Scale
Overall, Malaysia was one of the most crucial host countries of Chinese investments in SEA during 2005–19, accounting for 17 per cent of total Chinese investments in the region (CGIT data)—the third highest share among the ten SEA countries.

However, the pattern of Chinese investments in Malaysia during this period was episodic (see Figure 18). These investments more than quadrupled from US$1.8 billion in 2008 to a peak of US$7.8 billion in 2015. Moreover, the record high level of Chinese investments in Malaysia in 2015 was due to one cross-border transaction valued at US$5.26 billion: the acquisition by China General Nuclear Power Group of all energy assets owned by 1Malaysia Development Berhad (1MDB). After 2015, Chinese investments in Malaysia began to decline rapidly, from US$6.5 billion in 2016 to US$1.8 billion in 2019 (a level as low as that in 2008). In 2018–19, Chinese investments in Malaysia tumbled by almost 60 per cent from US$4.1 billion in 2018 to US$1.8 billion in 2019.

Relative Importance

Compared to other foreign investors, China was not a significant source of FDI in Malaysia for the most part during 2005–18.[44] As Table 10 shows, China's share of total FDI into Malaysia was no more than 3 per cent in each year between 2005 and 2018, except in 2016 (12 per cent) and 2017 (17 per cent). China's relatively high shares of total FDI in Malaysia in 2016 and 2017 corresponded roughly with the peak in Chinese investments in Malaysia discussed in the previous section. By comparison, the EU's share of total FDI in Malaysia generally exceeded 15 per cent during the same period, and those of Japan and the US were usually above 10 per cent. That being the case, only in three years during the fourteen-year period of 2005–18 was China among the top three non-ASEAN foreign investors in Malaysia: third in 2014, and second in 2016 and 2017. The increased relative importance of Chinese FDI in Malaysia in these three years was driven by a combination of increases in the absolute amounts of Chinese FDI, and decreases in other traditional sources of FDI—the latter likely due to the Najib government's huge 1MDB corruption scandal. For example, in 2016, Chinese FDI in Malaysia exceeded US$1.4 billion, more than four times its 2015 amount. But FDI from the EU (US$1.41 billion) and US (US$1.17 billion) was among

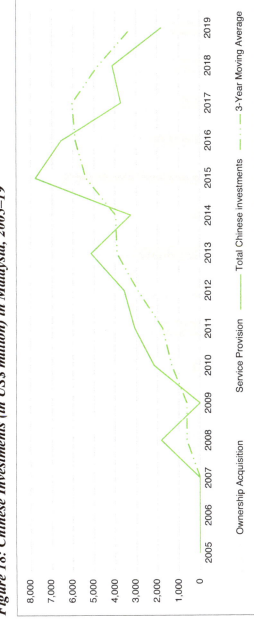

Figure 18: Chinese Investments (in US$ million) in Malaysia, 2005–19

Data Source: China Global Investment Tracker 2019 Fall Dataset (accessed in January 2020), China Global Investment Tracker 2021 Spring Dataset (accessed in August 2021).

Table 10: Top Three (Non-ASEAN) Foreign Investors in Malaysia, 2005–18

Year	Total	Largest Investor			Second Largest Investor			Third Largest Investor			Chinese FDI to Malaysia (in US$ million)	
		Investor	Amount	Share	Investor	Amount	Share	Investor	Amount	Share	Amount	Share
2005	4,064	US	1,368	34%	EU	961	24%	Japan	157	4%	1	0%
2006	6,060	Japan	2,849	47%	US	1,414	23%	EU	1,000	17%	−7	—
2007	8,401	EU	1,683	20%	Japan	887	11%	US	722	9%	5	0%
2008	8,053	US	1,467	18%	Japan	1,029	13%	EU	302	4%	57	1%
2009	1,405	EU	2,396	171%	Australia	182	13%	Japan	163	12%	−121	—
2010	9,156	US	2,492	27%	EU	1,980	22%	S. Korea	1,461	16%	−6	0%
2011	12,001	Japan	3,154	26%	EU	2,587	22%	US	1,172	10%	−15	—
2012	9,400	Japan	1,887	20%	EU	1,522	16%	Australia	539	6%	34	0%
2013	12,107	Japan	2,570	21%	EU	1,737	14%	US	187	2%	94	1%
2014	10,875	EU	2,984	27%	US	670	6%	China	302	3%	302	3%
2015	10,180	Japan	2,539	25%	US	1,491	15%	EU	1,377	14%	324	3%
2016	11,290	EU	1,410	12%	China	1,408	12%	US	1,174	10%	1,408	12%
2017	9,296	EU	2,366	25%	China	1,588	17%	Japan	1,164	13%	1,588	17%
2018	8,072	EU	2,236	28%	US	1,627	20%	Japan	1,194	15%	177	2%

Data Source: ASEAN Statistical Yearbooks.

their smallest FDI amounts during the 2005–18 period. Overall, the EU was among the top three non-ASEAN foreign investors in Malaysia every year, making it the largest source of FDI in Malaysia—the EU invested a total amount of US$24.5 billion during this fourteen-year period. Following the EU were Japan (about US$20 billion) and the US (about US$8.5 billion).

Distribution
Chinese investments in Malaysia were comparatively diversified across industrial sectors both in each individual year and across time during 2005–19 (see Figure 19). In no single year from 2008 to 2019 did China invest in only one industrial sector in Malaysia. Besides, each year the share of the industrial sector that received the largest amount of Chinese investments in Malaysia was not overwhelmingly high, generally sitting between 35 per cent and 65 per cent. Overall, the infrastructure sector accounted for the largest share of total Chinese investments in Malaysia during 2008–19, with an average share of 34 per cent. This was followed by the energy (27 per cent) and others (26 per cent) sectors. The metals sector had the lowest average share, at 13 per cent.

The *infrastructure* sector received a total of US$14.8 billion during 2005–19, nearly one-third of which was accounted for by Chinese investments in the East Coast Rail Link (ECRL) project in 2016 and 2018. Beyond that, in 2013, Guangxi Beibu Gulf International Port Group invested US$480 million to acquire 40 per cent ownership of Kuantan Port, a critical node in the ECRL. The multipurpose port is also linked to the Malaysia-China Kuantan Industrial Park, set up in the same year with 49 per cent ownership by a Chinese consortium led by the same investor. On the west coast of the Malay peninsula, in 2016, China also invested US$1.91 billion in the Melaka Gateway Port project.[45] Between 2008 and 2014, China invested a total of approximately US$3.17 billion in transport-related projects in the ethnic-Chinese dominant state of Penang, including a second road bridge, a road and seabed tunnel, three highways, and an underground tunnel linking the island to the peninsula. Apart from transport infrastructure, China

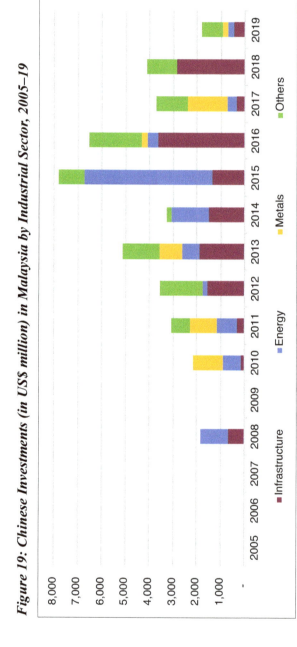

Figure 19: Chinese Investments (in US$ million) in Malaysia by Industrial Sector, 2005–19

Data Source: China Global Investment Tracker 2019 Fall Dataset (accessed in January 2020), China Global Investment Tracker 2021 Spring Dataset (accessed in August 2021).

invested US$1.42 billion in the Mersing Laguna tourism project in 2012, which included the construction of hotels, shopping malls, resorts, a marina and a theme park.[46]

The *energy* sector received an aggregate of US$11.7 billion, just about half of which was related to China's acquisition of 1MDB's energy assets in 2015, as discussed previously. Chinese investments in the *others* sector totalled US$11.1 billion, out of which nearly 40 per cent pertained to property investments and almost 25 per cent to tourism-related investments. China's total investments in Malaysia's *metals* sector during 2005–19 stood at US$5.5 billion, 57 per cent of which was invested in the steel industry. While Chinese investments in Malaysia's metals sector were relatively small compared to those in the other three industrial sectors in Malaysia, Malaysia's average share of Chinese metals investments in SEA between 2008 and 2019 was the second highest (at 19 per cent) among all SEA countries.

Laos

Absolute Scale

Having fluctuated significantly prior to 2012, Chinese investments in Laos exhibited a general increasing trend between 2012 and 2018, only to plummet in 2019 (see Figure 20). During 2005–11, while annual Chinese investments in Laos remained lower than US$300 million for the most part, they topped US$2 billion in 2007 and reached a new high of US$4.65 billion in 2010. The 2007 peak was driven by a construction contract (valued at US$1.7 billion) signed by Sinohydro and CEIEC (Chinese state-owned companies) to build the Pak Lay hydropower dam. Similarly, nearly two-thirds of the peak in 2010 was related to Chinese state-owned companies investing in Laos' energy sector. Starting from US$1.36 billion in 2012, Chinese investments in Laos more than quadrupled to US$5.93 billion in 2016 and reached a record high of US$7.42 billion in 2018. More than 70 per cent of Chinese investments in 2016 went to energy-related projects, with another 27 per cent going to an infrastructure project—China Railway

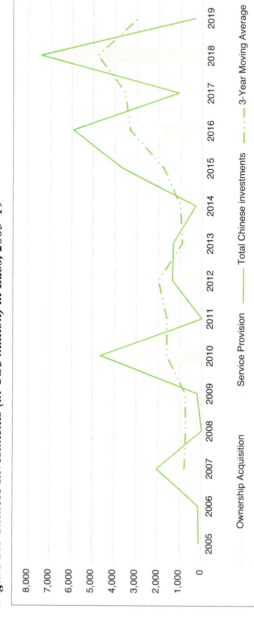

Figure 20: Chinese Investments (in US$ million) in Laos, 2005–19

Data Source: China Global Investment Tracker 2019 Fall Dataset (accessed in January 2020), China Global Investment Tracker 2021 Spring Dataset (accessed in August 2021).

Engineering's contract for work on the Boten-Vientiane railway. By comparison, infrastructure-related projects accounted for more than 70 per cent of Chinese investments in Laos in 2018, including the Kunming-Vientiane Railway project (valued at US$4.17 billion) and the Vientiane-Vangvieng Expressway project (valued at US$1.23 billion). Nevertheless, Chinese investments in Laos plunged to a mere US$350 million in 2019, one of the lowest levels during 2005–19. Overall, Laos received US$28.65 billion of Chinese investments in 2005–19, accounting for 11 per cent of total Chinese investments in SEA during this fifteen-year period (CGIT data).

Relative Importance
China was a significant source of FDI in Laos throughout 2005–18, and its significance noticeably increased after 2010 (see Table 11). Having remained as the second largest non-ASEAN foreign investor in Laos during 2005–8 (except in 2007), China became the largest foreign investor in Laos in 2009 and retained this position throughout until 2018 (except perhaps in 2012 and 2013 when data on FDI inflows to Laos by source country were not available). Notably, China's share of total annual FDI into Laos consistently exceeded 60 per cent from 2011 onwards and was even close to 80 per cent in 2017 and 2018. The rising relative importance of Chinese FDI in Laos could be attributed mainly to the absolute amount of Chinese FDI to Laos increasing significantly since 2011 while other FDI sources stagnated or declined. Chinese annual FDI multiplied from less than US$100 million in the pre-2011 period to more than US$1 billion in 2017 and 2018. In contrast, annual FDI from Japan and South Korea—two other main sources of FDI for Laos—only increased modestly during 2005–18. For example, Japanese FDI in Laos rose from under US$20 million in the pre-2011 period to less than US$80 million in the post-2011 period. Meanwhile, the EU, always among the top three foreign investors sources during 2005–10, has hardly counted among the top three since 2011. Overall, total Chinese FDI verged on US$5 billion in 2005–18—more than half of Laos' total FDI during this fourteen-

Table 11: Top Three (Non-ASEAN) Foreign Investors in Laos, 2005–18

Year	Total	Largest Investor			Second Largest Investor			Third Largest Investor			Chinese FDI to Laos (in US$ million)	
		Investor	Amount	Share	Investor	Amount	Share	Investor	Amount	Share	Amount	Share
2005	28	EU	8	28%	China	5	16%	Australia	4	15%	5	16%
2006	187	EU	158	84%	China	5	3%	US	1	1%	5	3%
2007	324	Japan	18	6%	EU	15	5%	S. Korea	15	5%	2	1%
2008	228	S. Korea	47	21%	China	43	19%	EU	10	4%	43	19%
2009	319	China	36	11%	Japan	14	4%	EU	11	3%	36	11%
2010	333	China	46	14%	EU	28	8%	Japan	8	2%	46	14%
2011	467	China	278	60%	Japan	12	3%	Russia	5	1%	278	60%
2012	294					N/A					N/A	
2013	427					N/A					N/A	
2014	913	China	614	67%	EU	51	6%	Australia	16	2%	614	67%
2015	1,079	China	665	62%	Japan	76	7%	S. Korea	46	4%	665	62%
2016	1,076	China	710	66%	S. Korea	77	7%	Japan	44	4%	710	66%
2017	1,695	China	1,314	77%	S. Korea	102	6%	Japan	70	4%	1,314	77%
2018	1,320	China	1,045	79%	Japan	48	4%	S. Korea	25	2%	1,045	79%

Data Source: ASEAN Statistical Yearbooks.

year period. By comparison, Japan, South Korea and the EU—the other three key sources—each accounted for less than 5 per cent.

Distribution
Chinese investments in Laos were concentrated mainly in the energy sector during 2005–19, with the infrastructure sector also accounting for sizeable shares in specific years (see Figure 21). Except in 2018, the *energy* sector had the largest share of Chinese investments in Laos among the four sectors being compared. With a total investment of US$16.77 billion, the energy sector constituted 59 per cent of overall Chinese investments in Laos during 2005–19. In 2005–7, 2009, 2013–14 and 2019, *all* Chinese investments in Laos went to the energy sector. During 2005–19, Laos took the second highest share (16.4 per cent) of total Chinese energy investments in SEA, second only to Indonesia (27.8 per cent). Notably, Chinese energy investments in Laos constituted roughly 40 per cent of total Chinese energy investments in SEA in 2007 and 2016.

   Nearly two-thirds of Chinese energy investments in Laos (approximately US$11 billion) went to hydropower projects. Some of the most valuable hydropower projects include the US$1.7 billion contract for the Pak Lay hydropower dam in Sainyabuli Province in 2007; a US$1.03 billion investment by Sinohydro to undertake the Nam Ngum 5 project in Luang Prabang and Xieng Khouang Provinces in 2010; and a US$2.03 billion investment by Chinese state-owned company Power Construction to develop the Nam Ou River Cascade in 2016. In addition, China invested US$3.78 billion in coal-related projects, including a US$1.68 billion contract in 2010 for Chinese state-owned company Sinomach to build the Hongsha Coal Power Plant in Northern Laos and another US$2.1 billion contract in 2016 for Sinomach to undertake a coal power integration project in Sekong Province.

   By comparison, Chinese *infrastructure* investments approximated US$8 billion in 2005–19, accounting for 28 per cent of total Chinese investments in Laos during this fifteen-year period. Notably, all Chinese infrastructure investments in Laos were made

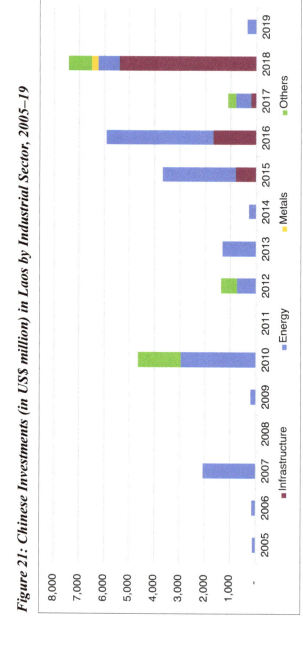

Figure 21: Chinese Investments (in US$ million) in Laos by Industrial Sector, 2005–19

Data Source: China Global Investment Tracker 2019 Fall Dataset (accessed in January 2020), China Global Investment Tracker 2021 Spring Dataset (accessed in August 2021).

between 2015 and 2018. The Kunming-Vientiane Railway was the most valuable Chinese infrastructure project in Laos; with a value of US$4.17 billion, the railway accounted for 56 per cent of total Chinese investments in the country in 2018. Other significant Chinese infrastructure projects include a US$1.58 billion contract in 2016 for China Railway Engineering to perform civil works on the Boten-Vientiane railway, and a US$1.23 billion contract in 2018 for Yunnan Construction Engineering to build an expressway linking Vientiane and Vangvieng.

While Chinese investments in the *others* sector in Laos accounted for 12 per cent of total Chinese investments in Laos during 2005–19 (equivalent to US$3.5 billion), the *metals* sector's share was a negligible 1 per cent during this fifteen-year period.

Vietnam

Absolute Scale
Chinese investments in Vietnam increased significantly in the late 2000s but declined steadily during the early 2010s, after which the investment amounts fluctuated widely (see Figure 22). Starting from less than US$800 million in 2006, Chinese investments in Vietnam more than quintupled to nearly US$4 billion in 2010, the highest level during 2005–19. Nearly 90 per cent of the US$4 billion investment in 2010 was in Vietnam's energy sector, with the largest cross-border transaction that year being a US$1.4 billion contract signed by Dongfang Electric Corporation for the first-phase construction of the offshore thermal power plant in Tra Vinh. Since 2010, Chinese investments in Vietnam followed a downward trend, touching a bottom of US$210 million in 2014. Following a temporary surge to US$3.5 billion in 2015 and dramatic drop to no large investments in 2016, Chinese investments in Vietnam fluctuated between US$1.2 billion (close to the 2008 level) and US$2.6 billion (similar to the 2009 level) in 2017–19. While the investment surge in both 2010 and 2015 pertained to Chinese investments in Vietnam's energy sector, the major transactions driving the 2015 surge involved Chinese

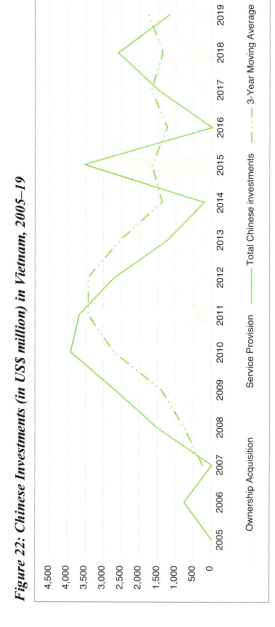

Figure 22: Chinese Investments (in US$ million) in Vietnam, 2005–19

Data Source: China Global Investment Tracker 2019 Fall Dataset (accessed in January 2020), China Global Investment Tracker 2021 Spring Dataset (accessed in August 2021).

acquisition of asset ownership in Vietnam rather than Chinese service provision, which was the case in 2010. Specifically, the two investments that contributed to the significant increase in 2015 were China Energy Engineering investing US$1.31 billion in two coal-fired plants in Hai Duong Province and Southern Power as well as State Power Investment investing US$1.76 billion in the Vinh Tan 1 power plant in Binh Thuan Province. Overall, Chinese investments in Vietnam totalled US$25.5 billion between 2005 and 2019, accounting for 10 per cent of total Chinese investments in SEA during this fifteen-year period (CGIT data). Nearly 80 per cent of the US$25.5 billion investments pertained to service provision (e.g., equipment installation and technical evaluation) by Chinese entities.

Relative Importance

Chinese FDI had limited relative importance in Vietnam during 2005–18. Accounting for 5 per cent of total FDI in Vietnam between 2005 and 2018, China was not considered to be among the top three non-ASEAN foreign investors in Vietnam (see Table 12). These were instead South Korea, Japan and the EU, which accounted for 20 per cent, 17 per cent and 8 per cent of total FDI in Vietnam respectively during 2005–18. That said, the relative importance of Chinese FDI in Vietnam increased moderately from 2013, with China being the third largest foreign investor in Vietnam for the most part during 2013–18. In particular, China accounted for 11 per cent of total FDI in Vietnam in 2013, the highest share for China during 2005–18. This increase in relative importance was due primarily to noticeable increases in Chinese FDI coupled with modest declines in FDI from the EU. Specifically, while Chinese FDI in Vietnam increased from an average of US$154 million during 2005–12 to an average of US$740 million during 2013–18, in the same period, the EU's FDI decreased from an average of US$778 million to an average of US$672 million. Nevertheless, the growth in Chinese investments was significant and probably under-reported in the ASEAN dataset used here. (The high levels of Chinese investments in Vietnam in 2009–12 discussed in the

Table 12: Top Three (Non-ASEAN) Foreign Investors in Vietnam, 2005–18

Year	Total	Largest Investor			Second Largest Investor			Third Largest Investor			Chinese FDI to Vietnam (in US$ million)	
		Investor	Amount	Share	Investor	Amount	Share	Investor	Amount	Share	Amount	Share
2005	2,021	EU	702	35%	US	260	13%	Japan	146	7%	48	2%
2006	2,400	S. Korea	484	20%	Japan	334	14%	EU	326	14%	89	4%
2007	6,739	S. Korea	1,358	20%	EU	901	13%	Japan	876	13%	252	4%
2008	8,050	Japan	971	12%	EU	872	11%	S. Korea	550	7%	45	1%
2009	7,600	US	3,307	44%	S. Korea	613	8%	EU	284	4%	112	1%
2010	8,000	EU	1,692	21%	S. Korea	1,336	17%	Japan	1,052	13%	115	1%
2011	7,519	Japan	1,248	17%	EU	900	12%	S. Korea	750	10%	383	5%
2012	8,368	Japan	2,863	34%	S. Korea	658	8%	EU	543	6%	190	2%
2013	8,900	Japan	2,365	27%	S. Korea	1,767	20%	China	948	11%	948	11%
2014	9,200	S. Korea	3,248	35%	Japan	969	11%	EU	552	6%	210	2%
2015	11,800	S. Korea	3,488	30%	EU	993	8%	Japan	955	8%	381	3%
2016	12,600	S. Korea	3,638	29%	Japan	1,339	11%	China	969	8%	969	8%
2017	14,100	Japan	3,580	25%	S. Korea	3,338	24%	China	852	6%	852	6%
2018	15,500	Japan	3,758	24%	S. Korea	3,152	20%	China	1,077	7%	1,077	7%

Data Source: ASEAN Statistical Yearbooks.

previous section were not fully reflected in the relative importance of Chinese FDI in Vietnam during this four-year period primarily because these large investments mainly took the form of Chinese service provision, which were not captured by the ASEAN Statistics dataset.) Overall, total Chinese FDI in Vietnam in 2005–18 approximated US$5.7 billion. By comparison, total FDI from South Korea, Japan and the EU during this fourteen-year period exceeded US$24 billion, US$20 billion and US$10 billion, respectively.

Distribution
Chinese investments in Vietnam were concentrated mainly in the energy sector, with the metals and others sectors also accounting for sizeable shares of Chinese investments in Vietnam in specific years (see Figure 23). China invested a total of US$15.9 billion in Vietnam's *energy* sector between 2005 and 2019, which accounted for nearly two-thirds of total Chinese investments in Vietnam during this fifteen-year period. This significant investment amount also resulted in Vietnam being the third largest recipient of total Chinese energy investments in SEA during 2005–19, with a share of 15.6 per cent (after Indonesia's share of 27.8 per cent and Laos' share of 16.4 per cent). Within the energy sector, more than 80 per cent of Chinese investments went to coal-related projects in Vietnam, whose total value approximated US$13 billion during 2005–19. Notably, the majority of the US$13 billion coal-related projects were located in Vietnam's southern provinces of Binh Thuan and Tra Vinh. By comparison, the *infrastructure* sector in Vietnam received US$3.8 billion in Chinese investments between 2005 and 2019, accounting for 15 per cent of total Chinese investments in Vietnam during this fifteen-year period. Following the infrastructure sector was the *metals* sector, where Chinese investments totalled US$3.2 billion during the same period. The most valuable Chinese metals investment in Vietnam pertained to a US$2.3 billion contract signed by Metallurgical Corporation of China in 2012 for the construction of facilities at a greenfield integrated steel mill in Ha Tinh Province. This US$2.3 billion

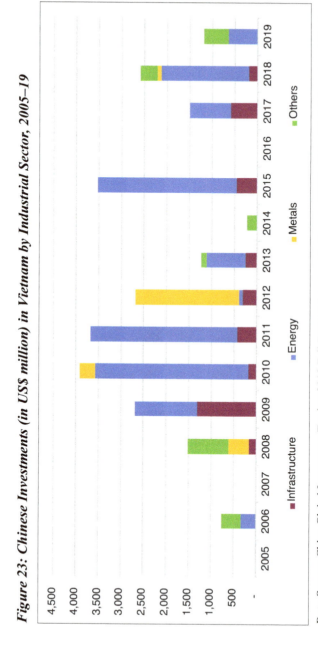

Figure 23: Chinese Investments (in US$ million) in Vietnam by Industrial Sector, 2005–19

Data Source: China Global Investment Tracker 2019 Fall Dataset (accessed in January 2020), China Global Investment Tracker 2021 Spring Dataset (accessed in August 2021).

contract, which was also the single largest Chinese investment in Vietnam between 2005 and 2019, resulted in Vietnam accounting for 55 per cent of total Chinese metals investments in SEA in 2012—the highest share among the ten SEA countries that year. Vietnam's *others* sector received the smallest amount (US$2.6 billion) of Chinese investments during 2005–19 among the four sectors being compared, accounting for 10 per cent of total Chinese investments in Vietnam during this fifteen-year period.

Cambodia

Absolute Scale

Chinese investments in Cambodia fluctuated around US$500 million during 2005–16, except in 2008, when the investment amount topped US$2.7 billion. After 2016, Chinese investments increased substantially, from US$1.4 billion in 2017 to US$4.4 billion in 2019 (see Figure 24). The investment peak in 2008 was attributed primarily to China's Tianjin Union Development Group investing US$1.5 billion to develop a tourism resort in Koh Kong. By comparison, the significant increases in Chinese investments in Cambodia during 2017–19 were due largely to rising Chinese investments in the infrastructure and energy sectors in Cambodia. For example, China Road and Bridge Corporation signed a US$2.08 billion contract in 2018 for the Phnom Penh-Sihanoukville Expressway Project, which accounted for two-thirds of total Chinese investments in Cambodia that year. In 2019, China Huadian Corporation invested US$1.19 billion in two coal-fired power units in Sihanoukville; this amount constituted more than one quarter of total Chinese investments in Cambodia in 2019. Overall, Chinese investments in Cambodia amounted to US$16.24 billion during 2005–19, which accounted for 6 per cent of total Chinese investments in SEA during this fifteen-year period (CGIT data).

Relative Importance

China was a crucial source of FDI in Cambodia between 2005

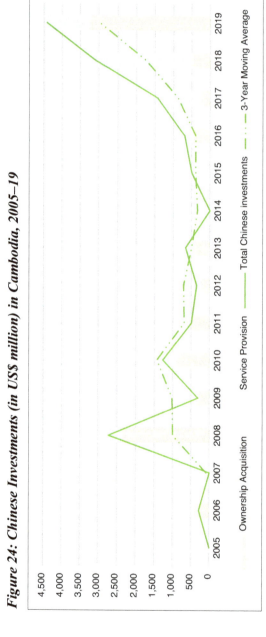

Figure 24: Chinese Investments (in US$ million) in Cambodia, 2005–19

Data Source: China Global Investment Tracker 2019 Fall Dataset (accessed in January 2020), China Global Investment Tracker 2021 Spring Dataset (accessed in August 2021).

and 2018. Except in 2008 and 2009, China was always the largest non-ASEAN foreign investor in Cambodia during 2005–18, and its share of total FDI in Cambodia was usually 10 percentage points higher than that of the second largest foreign investor in Cambodia (see Table 13). While South Korea overtook China as the largest foreign investor in Cambodia in 2008 and 2009, China's share of total FDI in Cambodia in 2009 (at 18.1 per cent) was very close to South Korea's share (at 18.2 per cent). By comparison, China's share of total FDI in Cambodia in 2008 (at 9 per cent) was roughly one-third of South Korea's share (at 25 per cent). China's record low share in 2008 was owing to both a substantial decrease in its FDI amount in Cambodia that year and a significant increase in South Korea's FDI amount. Specifically, China's FDI in Cambodia in 2008 stood at US$77 million, which was China's smallest annual FDI amount in Cambodia during 2005–18, whereas South Korea's FDI in Cambodia in the same year stood at US$203 million, which was South Korea's second highest annual FDI amount in Cambodia between 2005 and 2018. Overall, total Chinese FDI in Cambodia during 2005–18 exceeded US$4.5 billion, accounting for nearly one-quarter of total FDI in Cambodia during this fourteen-year period. Distantly following China were South Korea and the EU, whose FDI in Cambodia accounted for 9 per cent and 8 per cent respectively of total FDI in Cambodia during 2005–18.

Distribution
Chinese investments in Cambodia were concentrated primarily in the energy and others sectors prior to 2015 but shifted mainly towards the infrastructure sector from 2015 onwards (see Figure 25). Chinese investments in Cambodia's *energy* sector totalled US$2.79 billion between 2005 and 2014, which accounted for nearly half of total Chinese investments in Cambodia during this ten-year period. Almost three quarters of Chinese energy investments in Cambodia during 2005–14 pertained to hydropower projects. However, from 2015, Chinese energy investments in Cambodia shifted away from hydropower, and its share of total Chinese

Table 13: Top Three (Non-ASEAN) Foreign Investors in Cambodia, 2005–18

Year	Total	Largest Investor			Second Largest Investor			Third Largest Investor			Chinese FDI to Cambodia (in US$ million)	
		Investor	Amount	Share	Investor	Amount	Share	Investor	Amount	Share	Amount	Share
2005	381	China	103	27%	S. Korea	72	19%	Australia	24	6%	103	27%
2006	483	China	130	27%	US	51	10%	S. Korea	27	6%	130	27%
2007	867	China	165	19%	S. Korea	119	14%	EU	80	9%	165	19%
2008	815	S. Korea	203	25%	China	77	9%	EU	77	9%	77	9%
2009	539	S. Korea	98	18%	China	97	18%	India	28	5%	97	18%
2010	783	China	127	16%	S. Korea	47	6%	EU	43	6%	127	16%
2011	892	China	180	20%	S. Korea	139	16%	EU	54	6%	180	20%
2012	1,557	China	368	24%	S. Korea	162	10%	EU	126	8%	368	24%
2013	1,275	China	287	22%	S. Korea	178	14%	EU	116	9%	287	22%
2014	1,727	China	554	32%	EU	139	8%	S. Korea	106	6%	554	32%
2015	1,701	China	538	32%	EU	180	11%	S. Korea	72	4%	538	32%
2016	2,280	China	502	22%	Japan	199	9%	EU	194	9%	502	22%
2017	2,732	China	618	23%	Japan	227	8%	EU	214	8%	618	23%
2018	3,103	China	798	26%	S. Korea	250	8%	Japan	199	6%	798	26%

Data Source: ASEAN Statistical Yearbooks.

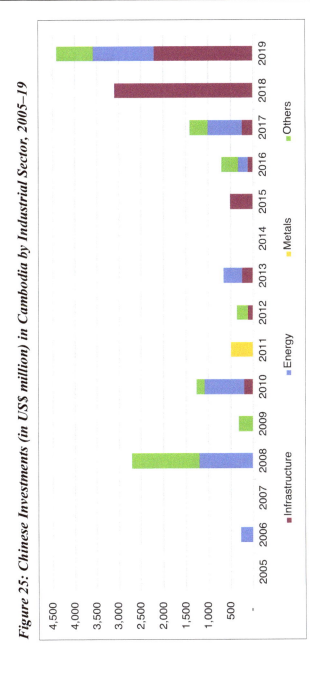

Figure 25: Chinese Investments (in US$ million) in Cambodia by Industrial Sector, 2005–19

Data Source: China Global Investment Tracker 2019 Fall Dataset (accessed in January 2020), China Global Investment Tracker 2021 Spring Dataset (accessed in August 2021).

investments in Cambodia decreased significantly, constituting less than one quarter of total Chinese investments in Cambodia between 2015 and 2019. Half of Chinese energy investments in Cambodia during 2015–19 were contributed by a single coal-related project—a US$1.19 billion investment by China Huadian Corporation in two coal-fired power units in Sihanoukville in 2019. This coal-related project was also the largest Chinese energy investment in Cambodia during 2005–19. Similar to the energy sector, the *others* sector's share of total Chinese investments in Cambodia halved from approximately one third of total Chinese investments in Cambodia during 2005–14 to 16 per cent during 2015–19. The US$1.5 billion tourism-related investment in 2008 by China's Tianjin Union Development Group, as discussed in the previous section, was a major contributor to the others sector's relatively high share of total Chinese investments in Cambodia during 2005–14.

By comparison, Chinese investments in Cambodia's *infrastructure* sector accounted for less than 10 per cent of total Chinese investments in Cambodia during 2005–14 but constituted more than 60 per cent (equivalent to US$6.19 billion) of total Chinese investments in Cambodia during 2015–19. The most valuable Chinese infrastructure investment in Cambodia between 2005 and 2019 pertained to the US$2.08 billion contract for the Phnom Penh-Sihanoukville Expressway Project signed by China Road and Bridge Corporation in 2018, which accounted for almost one third of total Chinese infrastructure investments in Cambodia during 2005–19. While Chinese investments in the aforementioned three sectors in Cambodia were spread across several years during 2005–19 (albeit to differing extents), Chinese investments in Cambodia's *metals* sector were concentrated in 2011 only. The US$500 million of Chinese metals investments in Cambodia in 2011 involved Guangxi Non-ferrous Metals Group investing in a steel plant and industrial zone in the Rovieng district of Preah Vihear Province.

Overall, China invested a total of US$6.76 billion in Cambodia's infrastructure sector between 2005 and 2019, which equalled

42 per cent of total Chinese investments in Cambodia during this fifteen-year period. Cambodia's energy sector, meanwhile, received US$5.15 billion in Chinese investments during the same period, accounting for approximately one third of total Chinese investments in Cambodia. Following the energy sector was the others sector, where Chinese investments totalled US$3.83 billion between 2005 and 2019 (equivalent to nearly one quarter of total Chinese investments in Cambodia during this fifteen-year period). Cambodia's metals sector received the smallest amount (US$500 million) of Chinese investments among the four sectors being compared, accounting for a mere 3 per cent of total Chinese investments in Cambodia during 2005–19.

The Philippines

Absolute Scale
Chinese investments in the Philippines fluctuated around US$800 million between 2008 and 2014 but exhibited an increasing trend from 2016, peaking at US$6.22 billion in 2019 (see Figure 26). The record in 2019 was contributed mainly by three transactions. The most valuable transaction of the three was Panhua Group's US$3.5 billion investment in an integrated steel plant in Misamis Oriental, which accounted for over half of total Chinese investments in the Philippines in 2019. Another important transaction in 2019 involved China Telecommunications Corporation investing US$760 million in Mislatel, the Philippines' third telecommunications service provider. The third key transaction in 2019 pertained to China Energy Engineering Corporation signing a US$800 million contract for the South Pulangi Hydroelectric Power Plant project. Notably, while total Chinese investments in the Philippines during 2005–19 were roughly equally split between investments involving ownership acquisition (at 45 per cent) and those involving service provision (at 55 per cent), nearly three quarters of the total investments involving ownership acquisition were contributed by two cross-border transactions, including the aforementioned US$3.5 billion metals investment

Figure 26: Chinese Investments (in US$ million) in the Philippines, 2005–19

Data Source: China Global Investment Tracker 2019 Fall Dataset (accessed in January 2020), China Global Investment Tracker 2021 Spring Dataset (accessed in August 2021).

by Panhua Group in 2019 and the US$1.58 billion investment by the State Grid Corporation of China in 2008 in the National Grid Corporation of the Philippines,[47] which holds a twenty-five-year franchise to operate and manage the power transmission facilities belonging to the Filipino government-owned National Transmission Corporation; by comparison, the two largest cross-border transactions involving service provision only accounted for roughly one third of the total investments involving service provision. Overall, according to CGIT data, China invested US$15.3 billion in the Philippines during 2005–19, accounting for 6 per cent of total Chinese investments in SEA during this fifteen-year period.

Relative Importance

China was an insignificant source of FDI in the Philippines during 2005–18, with China's share of total annual FDI in the Philippines being less than 3 per cent each year during this fourteen-year period (see Table 14). Throughout 2005–18, only in 2018 was China among the top three non-ASEAN foreign investors in the Philippines. China being the third largest foreign investor in the Philippines in 2018 was a result of both a significant increase in Chinese FDI in the Philippines in 2018 and substantial decreases in other traditional sources of FDI in the Philippines. Specifically, Chinese FDI in the Philippines in 2018 stood at US$199 million, which was China's largest annual FDI amount in the Philippines during 2005–18. In contrast, the EU's and Japan's FDI amounts in the Philippines in 2018, at US$340 million and US$219 million respectively, were among their lowest annual FDI levels in the Philippines during 2005–18. Overall, total Chinese FDI in the Philippines approximated US$350 million between 2005 and 2018, accounting for 1 per cent of total FDI in the Philippines during this fourteen-year period. By comparison, American FDI in the Philippines totalled US$10 billion during the same period, making the US the largest foreign investor in the Philippines. Following the US were Japan and the EU, which invested a total of US$6.2 billion and US$4.7 billion respectively in the Philippines between 2005 and 2018.

Table 14: Top Three (Non-ASEAN) Foreign Investors in the Philippines, 2005–18

Year	Total	Largest Investor			Second Largest Investor			Third Largest Investor			Chinese FDI to the Philippines (in US$ million)	
		Investor	Amount	Share	Investor	Amount	Share	Investor	Amount	Share	Amount	Share
2005	1,854	US	276	15%	Japan	61	3%	EU	45	2%	0	0%
2006	2,921	EU	418	14%	US	219	7%	Japan	55	2%	2	0%
2007	2,916	Japan	824	28%	US	655	22%	EU	89	3%	0	0%
2008	1,520	EU	455	30%	US	241	16%	Japan	56	4%	0	0%
2009	1,963	US	720	37%	Japan	591	30%	S. Korea	15	1%	−3	0%
2010	1,298	US	1,294	100%	Japan	18	1%	S. Korea	7	1%	0	0%
2011	1,816	US	578	32%	Japan	256	14%	S. Korea	21	1%	−4	0%
2012	2,797	US	871	31%	Australia	235	8%	EU	146	5%	−2	0%
2013	3,860	Japan	438	11%	S. Korea	47	1%	S. Korea	2	0%	6	0%
2014	5,815	US	2,307	40%	EU	577	10%	Japan	408	7%	47	1%
2015	5,639	US	1,791	32%	EU	1,183	21%	Japan	472	8%	59	1%
2016	8,280	Japan	2,727	33%	EU	1,672	20%	US	1,136	14%	17	0%
2017	10,256	EU	1,787	17%	US	473	5%	Japan	72	1%	29	0%
2018	9,832	EU	340	3%	Japan	219	2%	China	199	2%	199	2%

Data Source: ASEAN Statistical Yearbooks.

Distribution

As shown in Figure 27, Chinese investments in the Philippines were primarily in the energy sector during 2005–19, with significant investments made in the metals sector in 2019 and increasing investments going to the infrastructure sector from 2016 onwards. Specifically, Chinese *energy* investments in the Philippines amounted to US$8.74 billion during 2005–19, accounting for nearly 60 per cent of total Chinese investments in the Philippines during this fifteen-year period. The largest Chinese energy investment in the Philippines pertained to the US$1.58 billion investment made by the State Grid Corporation of China in 2008 to acquire 40 per cent ownership in the National Grid Corporation of the Philippines. This investment, which accounted for approximately one-fifth of total Chinese energy investments in SEA in 2008, was perceived to have granted China the potential ability to control the national electricity grid of the Philippines. Other significant Chinese energy investments in the Philippines include two coal-related projects. One project involved a US$1 billion contract signed by Power Construction Corporation of China in 2014 to build a thermal facility in Kauswagan, Lanao del Norte. The other project was a US$1.67 billion contract signed by China Communications Construction Company and Power Construction Corporation of China in 2017 to build a coal-fired power plant in Dinginin, Bataan. China invested a total of US$3.5 billion in the *metals* sector in the Philippines between 2005 and 2019, which accounted for almost one quarter of total Chinese investments in the Philippines during this fifteen-year period. Notably, the US$3.5 billion metals investments were contributed by a single transaction—Panhua Group's investment in an integrated steel plant in Misamis Oriental in 2019. This significant metals investment also resulted in the Philippines accounting for more than half of total Chinese metals investments in SEA in 2019—the highest share among the ten SEA countries that year. Chinese *infrastructure* investments in the Philippines totalled US$2.86 billion between 2005 and 2019, accounting for roughly one-fifth of total Chinese investments in the Philippines

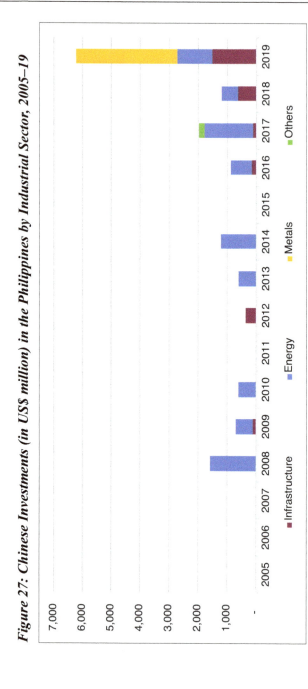

Figure 27: Chinese Investments (in US$ million) in the Philippines by Industrial Sector, 2005–19

Data Source: China Global Investment Tracker 2019 Fall Dataset (accessed in January 2020), China Global Investment Tracker 2021 Spring Dataset (accessed in August 2021).

during this fifteen-year period. Approximately 85 per cent of the US$2.86 billion Chinese infrastructure investments in the Philippines were made during 2016–19. The most valuable Chinese infrastructure investment in the Philippines pertained to China Telecommunications Corporation investing US$860 million in 2019 in Mislatel, the Philippines' third telecommunications service provider. The *others* sector received US$190 million in Chinese investments during 2005–19, constituting a mere 1 per cent of total Chinese investments in the Philippines during this fifteen-year period.

Thailand

Absolute Scale
Chinese annual investments in Thailand remained below US$1.5 billion between 2005 and 2019, except in 2018, when the investment amount reached US$4.16 billion—the highest level of Chinese investments in Thailand during this fifteen-year period (see Figure 28). Nearly two-thirds of the US$4.16 billion Chinese investment in 2018 pertained to the US$2.69 billion contract signed by China Railway Construction Corporation Limited and China Railway Engineering Corporation for undertaking the Thailand-China railway project. This contract was the largest Chinese investment in Thailand between 2005 and 2019. While Chinese investments in Thailand generally remained low during 2005–19, the level of investments during 2014–19 (largely fluctuating around US$1 billion) was roughly three times that during 2009–13 (largely fluctuating around US$300 million). Overall, according to CGIT data, Chinese investments in Thailand totalled US$11.6 billion between 2005 and 2019, accounting for 5 per cent of total Chinese investments in SEA during this fifteen-year period.

Relative Importance
China was not a significant source of FDI in Thailand during 2005–18, accounting for a mere 3 per cent of total FDI in Thailand

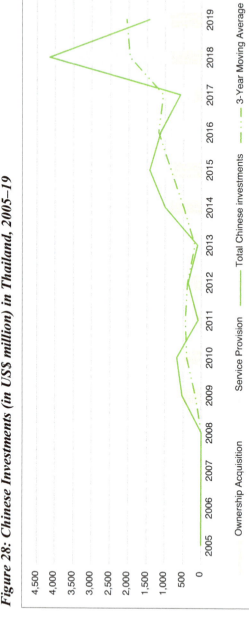

Figure 28: Chinese Investments (in US$ million) in Thailand, 2005–19

Data Source: China Global Investment Tracker 2019 Fall Dataset (accessed in January 2020), China Global Investment Tracker 2021 Spring Dataset (accessed in August 2021).

during this fourteen-year period. Only in four years between 2005 and 2018 was China among the top three non-ASEAN foreign investors in Thailand (see Table 15). This is in stark contrast to Japan, which was almost always the largest foreign investor in Thailand between 2005 and 2018. The US and EU were also usually among the largest three foreign investors in Thailand. Even when China was among the top three foreign investors in Thailand, its share was generally in single digits and much lower than those of the other top foreign investors in Thailand. For example, China was the third largest foreign investor in Thailand in 2006 but only accounted for a negligible 1 per cent of total FDI in Thailand that year. By comparison, Japan and the EU—the other two of the top three foreign investors in Thailand in 2006— accounted for 27 per cent and 10 per cent respectively of total FDI in Thailand. However, in 2016, China's share of total FDI in Thailand verged on 40 per cent, the highest share for China during 2005–18. This high share could be attributed partly to an increase in China's absolute amount of FDI in Thailand in 2016 and, to a greater extent, to decreases in other traditional sources of FDI in Thailand that year. Specifically, China's FDI in Thailand exceeded US$1 billion in 2016, China's largest annual FDI amount in Thailand during 2005–18. In contrast, the EU divested more than US$4 billion from Thailand in 2016, and the US invested one of its smallest FDI amounts (at US$439 million) in Thailand that year. Overall, Japan was the most significant source of FDI in Thailand between 2005 and 2018, whose total FDI amount exceeded US$47 billion, accounting for nearly 40 per cent of total FDI in Thailand during this fourteen-year period. The US and EU were a distant second and third, accounting for 9 per cent and 5 per cent respectively of total FDI in Thailand.

Distribution
Chinese investments in Thailand were concentrated over-whelmingly in the others sector prior to 2012 but shifted primarily towards the infrastructure sector from 2012 onwards (see Figure 29). The *infrastructure* sector received the largest amount

Table 15: Top Three (Non-ASEAN) Foreign Investors in Thailand, 2005–18

Year	Total	Largest Investor			Second Largest Investor			Third Largest Investor			Chinese FDI to Thailand (in US$ million)	
		Investor	Amount	Share	Investor	Amount	Share	Investor	Amount	Share	Amount	Share
2005	8,048	Japan	2,927	36%	EU	335	4%	China	12	0%	12	0%
2006	9,460	Japan	2,576	27%	EU	960	10%	China	50	1%	50	1%
2007	11,238	Japan	3,136	28%	EU	1,581	14%	S. Korea	390	3%	74	1%
2008	9,835	Japan	2,532	26%	US	1,018	10%	EU	791	8%	69	1%
2009	6,412	Japan	1,535	24%	EU	980	15%	Canada	794	12%	169	3%
2010	14,747	Japan	4,400	30%	US	1,431	10%	EU	1,276	9%	633	4%
2011	2,474	EU	843	34%	US	143	6%	S. Korea	97	4%	21	1%
2012	12,899	US	3,967	31%	Japan	3,707	29%	Canada	2,352	18%	599	5%
2013	15,936	Japan	10,927	69%	China	939	6%	US	857	5%	939	6%
2014	4,976	Japan	2,431	49%	US	2,023	41%	Canada	901	18%	–221	N/A
2015	8,928	Japan	3,006	34%	US	1,083	12%	EU	1,065	12%	238	3%
2016	2,810	Japan	2,986	106%	China	1,072	38%	US	439	16%	1,072	38%
2017	8,229	Japan	3,132	38%	EU	711	9%	S. Korea	168	2%	73	1%
2018	13,205	Japan	5,251	40%	EU	1,539	12%	US	810	6%	662	5%

Data Source: ASEAN Statistical Yearbooks.

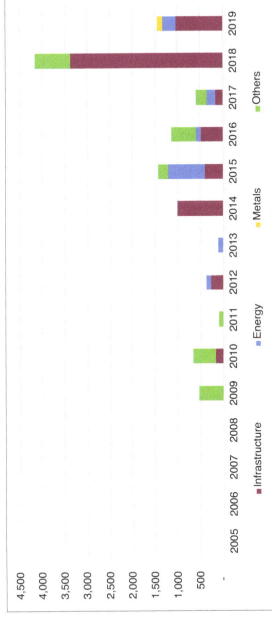

Figure 29: Chinese Investments (in US$ million) in Thailand by Industrial Sector, 2005–19

Data Source: China Global Investment Tracker 2019 Fall Dataset (accessed in January 2020), China Global Investment Tracker 2021 Spring Dataset (accessed in August 2021).

of Chinese investments in Thailand—at US$6.91 billion—during 2005–19 among the four sectors being compared. The most valuable was the US$2.69 billion contract for the Thailand-China railway project, which accounted for nearly 40 per cent of total Chinese infrastructure investments in Thailand between 2005 and 2019. Other important Chinese infrastructure investments in Thailand include China Mobile acquiring 18 per cent stake in Thai telecoms group True Corp in 2014 (at a price of US$880 million) and China Railway Construction Corporation investing US$740 million in a US$7.4 billion agreement in 2019 to build a high-speed rail network linking Suvarnabhumi Airport with Don Mueang International Airport and U-Tapao International Airport. Following the infrastructure sector was the *others* sector, which received approximately US$3 billion of Chinese investments during 2005–19. Within the others sector, Chinese investments were roughly evenly spread across the property, agriculture, chemicals, finance and consumer sectors. Chinese *energy* investments in Thailand totalled US$1.6 billion between 2005 and 2019, which was the third largest amount received among the four sectors being compared. Approximately half of Chinese energy investments in Thailand during 2005–19 were made in 2015, and the largest Chinese energy investment in Thailand involved Zhongli Talesun Solar investing US$300 million in new 800MW Cell & Module highly automated manufacturing facilities in Rayong. The *metals* sector in Thailand received US$130 million of Chinese investments during 2005–19, which was the smallest amount among the four sectors being compared. Overall, the infrastructure sector accounted for 60 per cent of total Chinese investments in Thailand between 2005 and 2019, followed by the others sector (25 per cent), energy sector (14 per cent) and metals sector (1 per cent) respectively.

Myanmar

Absolute Scale
Chinese investments in Myanmar totalled US$9.6 billion during

2005–19. While Chinese investments in Myanmar did not exhibit a clear pattern (see Figure 30), the investments during 2008–10 and 2016–18 constituted almost 90 per cent of total Chinese investments in Myanmar during 2005–19. In particular, the year 2016 witnessed US$2.65 billion in Chinese investments—the highest level during this fifteen-year period. Nearly 80 per cent of the US$2.65 billion investment in 2016 pertained to Zhuhai Zhenrong, one of the four licensed state importers of crude oil in China, constructing an oil refinery in Dawei (with a capacity of 100,000 barrels per day). Further details about the oil refinery project in Dawei will be provided in the *Distribution* section below. Apart from 2016, Chinese investments in 2009, 2010 and 2018 also surpassed the US$1 billion benchmark. The amount aside, Chinese investments in Myanmar were consistently dominated by acquisitions of asset ownership. Specifically, nearly 70 per cent of Chinese investments in Myanmar between 2005 and 2019 involved Chinese entities acquiring asset ownership in this SEA host country. Overall, Chinese investments in Myanmar accounted for 4 per cent of total Chinese investments in SEA during 2005–19 (CGIT data).

Relative Importance
While Myanmar did not account for a sizeable share of Chinese investments in SEA, China was a significant source of FDI in Myanmar between 2005 and 2018. During this fourteen-year period, China was always among the top three non-ASEAN foreign investors in Myanmar, and for half of the time, the largest foreign investor in Myanmar (see Table 16). China's share of total FDI in Myanmar was most significant between 2008 and 2013, accounting for an average of 40 per cent of total FDI in Myanmar. This increasing relative importance of Chinese FDI in Myanmar was due primarily to rising absolute amounts of Chinese FDI in Myanmar, from an average of less than US$2 million during 2005–7 to an average of US$700 million during 2008–13. In particular, China accounted for 68 per cent of total FDI in Myanmar in 2010, the highest share for any largest foreign investor

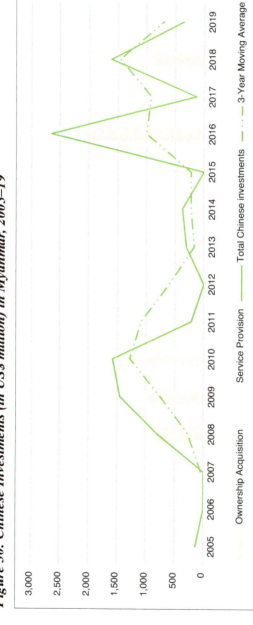

Figure 30: Chinese Investments (in US$ million) in Myanmar, 2005–19

Data Source: China Global Investment Tracker 2019 Fall Dataset (accessed in January 2020), China Global Investment Tracker 2021 Spring Dataset (accessed in August 2021).

Table 16: Top Three (Non-ASEAN) Foreign Investors in Myanmar, 2005–18

Year	Total	Largest Investor			Second Largest Investor			Third Largest Investor			Chinese FDI to Myanmar (in US$ million)	
		Investor	Amount	Share	Investor	Amount	Share	Investor	Amount	Share	Amount	Share
2005	236	EU	135	57%	Australia	2	1%	China	1	1%	1	1%
2006	428	EU	181	42%	S. Korea	120	28%	China	2	0%	2	0%
2007	258	S. Korea	103	40%	EU	85	33%	China	2	1%	2	1%
2008	715	China	349	49%	EU	183	26%	S. Korea	13	2%	349	49%
2009	963	China	371	38%	EU	98	10%	NZ	65	7%	371	38%
2010	2,249	China	1,521	68%	EU	215	10%	India	14	1%	1,521	68%
2011	2,058	China	671	33%	EU	369	18%	US	103	5%	671	33%
2012	1,354	EU	664	49%	China	482	36%	Japan	31	2%	482	36%
2013	2,621	China	793	30%	EU	296	11%	Japan	36	1%	793	30%
2014	946	China	71	7%	Japan	38	4%	Japan	28	3%	71	7%
2015	2,825	EU	203	7%	Japan	95	3%	China	52	2%	52	2%
2016	2,990	EU	839	28%	China	206	7%	US	43	1%	206	7%
2017	4,002	China	554	14%	EU	447	11%	Japan	208	5%	554	14%
2018	1,610	Japan	289	18%	EU	177	11%	China	75	5%	75	5%

Data Source: ASEAN Statistical Yearbooks.

in Myanmar between 2005 and 2018. This sizeable share could be attributed mainly to the US$1.02 billion Kyaukphyu oil-gas pipeline project invested by China National Petroleum Corporation in 2009, which, due probably to different data recording timings, was reflected in China's share of FDI in Myanmar in 2010. As the average absolute amount of Chinese FDI in Myanmar decreased to less than US$200 million during 2014–18, China's relative importance as a source of FDI in Myanmar declined accordingly, to an average share of 7 per cent. Overall, China accounted for 22 per cent of total FDI in Myanmar during 2005–18. Following China was the EU, which accounted for 17 per cent of total FDI in Myanmar during this fourteen-year period. Japan was a distant third, accounting for a mere 3 per cent.

Distribution

Chinese investments in Myanmar were relatively diversified across the energy, infrastructure and metals sectors during 2005–19, but were substantially concentrated in one of the three industrial sectors in a single year (see Figure 31). The *energy* sector accounted for 100 per cent of Chinese investments in Myanmar in 2005, 2009, 2014 as well as 2017 and 88 per cent in 2016. As mentioned previously, the most valuable Chinese energy investment in Myanmar was the construction by Zhuhai Zhenrong of an oil refinery in Dawei. This US$2.1 billion oil refinery project, which could facilitate the refining of oil imported from the Middle East, was perceived as fitting well into China's Maritime Silk Road initiative and as China challenging Japan's and Thailand's interests in the Special Economic Zone in Dawei. Another significant Chinese energy investment in Myanmar pertained to the US$1.02 billion Kyaukphyu oil-gas pipeline project. This pipeline project, whose initial blueprint dated back to the early 2000s, was believed to be able to deliver a range of economic, strategic and geo-political benefits to China. Meanwhile, Chinese *infrastructure* investments in Myanmar concentrated primarily in 2011, 2013, 2018 and 2019, accounting for an average of nearly 90 per cent of total Chinese investments in Myanmar these four years. The US$910 million

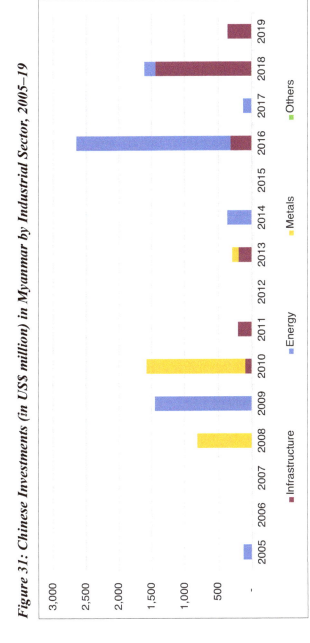

Figure 31: Chinese Investments (in US$ million) in Myanmar by Industrial Sector, 2005–19

Data Source: China Global Investment Tracker 2019 Fall Dataset (accessed in January 2020), China Global Investment Tracker 2021 Spring Dataset (accessed in August 2021).

deep-sea port at Kyaukphyu, invested by a consortium led by
Chinese state-owned investment company CITIC Group, was the
most significant Chinese infrastructure investment in Myanmar
during 2005–19. This deep-sea port project is closely related to the
Kyaukphyu oil-gas pipeline project and, together with an industrial
park, forms the Special Economic Zone being developed by China
in Kyaukphyu. By comparison, the *metals* sector accounted for
100 per cent and 94 per cent of Chinese investments in Myanmar
in 2008 and 2010, respectively. The sizeable Chinese metals
investments in both 2008 and 2010 were in Sagaing Region of
Myanmar. Specifically, the 2008 investment was relating to state-
owned China Nonferrous Metal Mining Group investing US$810
million in the Tagaung Taung Nickel Mine Project, and the 2010
investment pertaining to state-owned Norinco investing US$1.48
billion in the Letpadaung Copper Mine Project. Notably, Chinese
metals investments in Myanmar in 2008 and 2010 accounted for
64 per cent and 48 per cent of total Chinese metals investments in
SEA these two years respectively, the highest shares among the
ten SEA countries in respective years. Overall, the energy sector
received approximately US$4.6 billion Chinese investments
between 2005 and 2019, accounting for nearly 50 per cent of total
Chinese investments in Myanmar during this fifteen-year period.
Following the energy sector was the infrastructure sector, with a
total investment amount of US$2.63 billion and a share of 27 per
cent. The metals sector received a similar investment amount
(US$2.39 billion) to the infrastructure sector and accounted for
25 per cent of total Chinese investments in Myanmar during
2005–19.

Brunei

Absolute Scale
Chinese investments in Brunei were sporadic during 2005–19,
with more than 80 per cent of total Chinese investments in Brunei
during this fifteen-year period concentrated in 2014 alone (see
Figure 32). The substantial Chinese investment in Brunei in 2014,

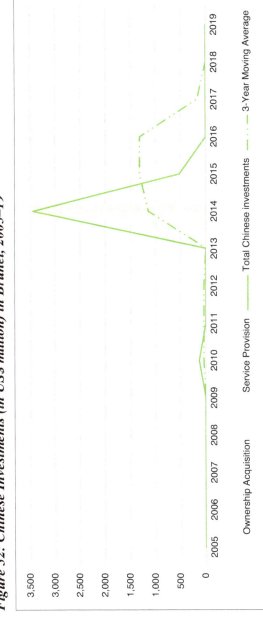

Figure 32: Chinese Investments (in US$ million) in Brunei, 2005–19

Data Source: China Global Investment Tracker 2019 Fall Dataset (accessed in January 2020), China Global Investment Tracker 2021 Spring Dataset (accessed in August 2021).

at US$3.44 billion, pertained to Zhejiang Hengyi Group investing in Phase 1 of an oil refinery and petrochemical complex project at Pulau Muara Besar.[48] Another project that China undertook at Pulau Muara Besar related to a US$200 million contract signed by China Communications Construction in 2015 to construct the Pulau Muara Besar Bridge, connecting west Brunei's Muara with east Brunei's Pulau Muara Besar. Overall, China invested approximately US$4 billion in Brunei between 2005 and 2019, accounting for 2 per cent of total Chinese investments in SEA during this fifteen-year period (CGIT data).

Relative Importance
China was an insignificant source of FDI in Brunei between 2005 and 2018. During this fourteen-year period, only in 2018 was China among the top three non-ASEAN foreign investors in Brunei (see Table 17). Even when China was the second largest foreign investor in Brunei in 2018, its share of total FDI in Brunei that year was negligible (close to 0 per cent) and well below the share of Japan (at 12 per cent), which was the largest foreign investor in Brunei in 2018. Overall, Chinese FDI in Brunei totalled US$25 million between 2005 and 2018. By comparison, the EU's FDI in Brunei exceeded US$3 billion during 2005–18, accounting for nearly half of total FDI in Brunei during this fourteen-year period. Distantly following the EU were Japan and the US, whose total FDI in Brunei approximated US$500 million and US$100 million respectively between 2005 and 2018.

Distribution
Chinese investments in Brunei were concentrated in the energy and infrastructure sectors during 2005–19, with the former accounting for 84 per cent of total Chinese investments in Brunei during this fifteen-year period and the latter accounting for 16 per cent (see Figure 33). As mentioned before, the sizeable Chinese *energy* investments in Brunei related to Zhejiang Hengyi Group investing US$3.44 billion in 2014 in Phase 1 of an oil refinery and petrochemical complex project at Pulau Muara Besar. This

Table 17: Top Three (Non-ASEAN) Foreign Investors in Brunei, 2005–18

Year	Total	Largest Investor			Second Largest Investor			Third Largest Investor			Chinese FDI to Brunei (in US$ million)	
		Investor	Amount	Share	Investor	Amount	Share	Investor	Amount	Share	Amount	Share
2005	289	EU	200	69%	S. Korea	23	8%	Japan	20	7%	0	0%
2006	434	EU	303	70%	Japan	35	8%	US	32	7%	5	1%
2007	260	Japan	77	29%	EU	38	14%	US	20	8%	17	7%
2008	239	EU	231	97%	Japan	6	2%	US	1	0%	N/A	N/A
2009	371	EU	296	80%	Japan	64	17%	US	5	1%	0	0%
2010	625	EU	448	72%	Japan	48	8%	US	33	5%	0	0%
2011	1,208	EU	984	81%	Japan	127	10%	US	27	2%	0	0%
2012	865	EU	615	71%	Japan	56	6%	US	32	4%	0	0%
2013	726	EU	602	83%	Canada	26	4%	Japan	16	2%	0	0%
2014	568	EU	367	65%	Canada	61	11%	Japan	27	5%	0	0%
2015	171	EU	84	49%	Canada	1	0%	N/A	N/A	N/A	0	0%
2016	–150	US	2	N/A	Australia	1	N/A	Canada	1	N/A	0	0%
2017	460				N/A						0	0%
2018	504	Japan	63	12%	China	2	0%	Canada	2	0%	2	0%

Data Source: ASEAN Statistical Yearbooks.

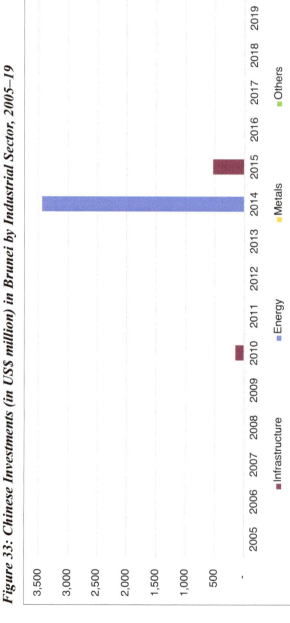

Figure 33: Chinese Investments (in US$ million) in Brunei by Industrial Sector, 2005–19

Data Source: China Global Investment Tracker 2019 Fall Dataset (accessed in January 2020), China Global Investment Tracker 2021 Spring Dataset (accessed in August 2021).

investment constituted nearly 40 per cent of total Chinese energy investments in SEA in 2014. In contrast, Chinese *infrastructure* projects in Brunei were on a much smaller scale. The largest of these pertained to a US$330 million contract signed by China State Construction Engineering Corporation in 2015 to construct the Sultan Haji Omar Ali Saifuddien Bridge, which links the Brunei-Muara district with the Temburong district. The other two Chinese infrastructure projects in Brunei involved China Communications Construction signing a US$140 million contract in 2010 to build a highway linking Telisai with Lumut, and another US$200 million contract in 2015 to construct the Pulau Muara Besar Bridge connecting Muara with Pulau Muara Besar. Overall, China invested US$3.44 billion in Brunei's energy sector during 2005–19 and US$670 million in Brunei's infrastructure sector during the same period.

APPENDIX

A1. Selection of Datasets on Chinese Investments in Southeast Asia

This report surveys key changes in Chinese investments in SEA economies since the mid-2000s (following from the Chinese government's 1999 "Going Global" strategy). To achieve this research objective, we examined various databases on Chinese overseas investments, including:

- China Global Investment Tracker (CGIT) database;
- ASEAN Statistical Yearbooks;
- Foreign direct investment (FDI) data compiled by the World Bank;
- FDI data compiled by the International Monetary Fund (IMF);
- FDI data compiled by the Asian Development Bank;
- Statistical Bulletin of China's Outward FDI released by China's Ministry of Commerce;
- Data on China's outward direct investment released by China's Bureau of Statistics;
- Global Chinese Official Finance Dataset, 2000–2014, Version 1.0; and
- China Global Energy Finance database.

We eventually decided to use the CGIT database as the primary data source for this project for three reasons. First, unlike other datasets on Chinese investment which are either too aggregated or too segmented,[49] CGIT provides up-to-date data on Chinese investments in each SEA country by industrial sector over a reasonably long period, from 2005 to 2019 (as at the time when data analysis first commenced in early 2020[50]). This allowed us to examine the industry-specific trends and patterns of Chinese investments in every SEA country over the past fifteen years and to compare the features of Chinese investments across SEA countries. Section A4 of this Appendix explains how we selected and classified industrial sectors for this project. Second, the CGIT database includes two broad types of Chinese investments— transactions involving Chinese acquisition of asset ownership, and Chinese provision of services, in SEA countries. These two classifications enabled us to further disaggregate the relative spread of types of investments across SEA countries and industrial sectors. Third, the CGIT database provides additional information about investors and other transaction parties, facilitating our identification of specific Chinese investments that were of significance or particular interest. The CGIT database is a public dataset compiled and published by the American Enterprise Institute and the Heritage Foundation in the United States.[51]

However, it is important to note that the CGIT database only tracks "large" investments worth at least US$100 million. For the purposes of our larger project—which investigates the relationship between Chinese investment and domestic politics (especially the security and legitimacy of ruling regimes)—this data is most suitable because it captures the major Chinese investments that are most politically visible and/or are most mobilizable for political purposes. But it does mean that our analysis does not capture smaller Chinese investments in SEA countries. In the main, we do not regard this as problematic; however, we are aware that smaller Chinese investments may have a significant cumulative effect in the countries that attract relatively small total amounts of FDI. Therefore, we provide some contextualization of the large Chinese investments against the overall figures for inward-FDI into the individual SEA countries, and against China's total FDI in each country. We also compare China's total FDI against those of the top three FDI sources for each country. To provide this context, we used the ASEAN Statistical Yearbooks—published by the Secretariat of the Association of Southeast Asian Nations (ASEAN Secretariat)[52]—as a complementary data source.[53] ASEAN Statistical Yearbooks provide data on FDI inflows into each SEA country by major source country, from 1995 to 2018 (as at the time when data analysis first commenced in early 2020[54]). The ASEAN Statistical Yearbooks also allowed us to roughly cross-check the general trends of Chinese investments in SEA countries during the period of 2005 to 2018. We noted and managed some inherent data discrepancies between the ASEAN Statistical Yearbooks and the CGIT database, as explained below in section A5 of this Appendix.

In summary, for this project, the CGIT database was used for discussions about the absolute level and industry-sector distribution of large Chinese investments in SEA countries, and the ASEAN Statistical Yearbooks for discussions about the relative importance of overall Chinese FDI in SEA countries vis-à-vis other investing countries.

A2. Defining "Chinese Investments": CGIT Database vs ASEAN Statistical Yearbooks

While these two data sources both include Chinese investments from state-owned and private entities in their data compilation, the CGIT database and ASEAN Statistical Yearbooks use different geo-allocation principles to determine what is considered "Chinese". Specifically, the CGIT database uses the "ultimate parent company" principle to decide if an investment would be recorded as "Chinese" investments. This means that investments from Mainland Chinese parent companies' subsidiaries, regardless of whether the subsidiaries are located/incorporated in Mainland China, would be recorded as "Chinese" investments, whereas investments from non-Mainland Chinese parent companies' subsidiaries, even if the subsidiaries are located/incorporated in Mainland China, would not be recorded as "Chinese" investments. In contrast, ASEAN Statistical Yearbooks mainly uses the "immediate investing country" principle to determine if an investment would be recorded as "Chinese" investments. This means that investments from Mainland Chinese parent companies' subsidiaries that are not located/incorporated in Mainland China would not be recorded as "Chinese" investments, whereas investments from non-Mainland Chinese parent companies' subsidiaries that are located/incorporated in Mainland China would be recorded as "Chinese" investments.

The CGIT database and ASEAN Statistical Yearbooks also adopt differing monetary and ownership thresholds to determine what types of Chinese investments would be included in their data collection. See section A5 below.

Bearing in mind the aforementioned differences in how "Chinese investments" are defined in the CGIT database and ASEAN Statistical Yearbooks, the wording "Chinese investments" was used in this report when discussing analysis based on CGIT data, whereas the wording "Chinese FDI" was used when discussing analysis based on ASEAN Statistical Yearbooks.

A3. Definition of "Investment"

In this report, we use "investment" to refer to Chinese investment, project financing, and service provision in SEA.

The CGIT dataset that our report relies on captures the two key forms of Foreign Direct Investment (mergers & acquisitions or M&A, and greenfield investment), *as well as* other forms of cross-border investment flows that tend to be tightly associated with Chinese investments in SEA. In particular, construction contracts (in-country services) are a significant element of Chinese overseas economic activity in developing countries that accompanies investment, but can also be a form of trade in services that is even more significant than M&A.

From 2020, UNCTAD also began noting in its annual *World Investment Report* that a general category of what it terms "project finance" "is a significant part of cross-border investment flows", most of which concerns investment in infrastructure:

> Project finance can be purely domestic or international. It is a form of FDI when foreign sponsors participate in the equity of a project company at shares of more than 10 per cent. The project

company set up to carry out the project is usually financed with a loan structure that relies primarily on the project's cash flow for repayment, with the project's assets, rights and interests held as secondary collateral. The financing of the project company can involve a combination of MNEs and commercial lenders, as well as public sector partners, such as bilateral and multilateral donors, regional development banks and export credit agencies.[55]

We note that this "project financing" category of investment flows appears to be designed to take into account not just China's overseas infrastructure investments, but similar forms of investment that rival schemes—such as the Blue Dot Network, or Partnership for Quality Infrastructure—seek to provide.

M&A, greenfield investment and project finance are all covered under the "ownership" data in CGIT. The "service provision" data supplements (and may slightly overlap with) these forms of foreign direct investment. We recognize that "service provision" is, technically, trade in services rather than investment. However, we include this data in our study to reflect the integral part construction contracts, for example, play in key Chinese project financing in SEA, especially in the infrastructure and energy sectors. For example, many very large Chinese-financed hydropower projects in the region are funded under a "build-operate-transfer" (BOT) arrangement, whereby ownership of the asset transfers back into the host state's hands after an agreed period (usually twenty to thirty years). Thus, such projects might initially be categorized as Chinese construction contracts rather than as acquisition-based investments. However, the Chinese consortia or enterprises essentially own, operate, and try to maximize profits from the asset for the initial period of time.

More generally, this intertwining of FDI and service provision is characteristic of what political economists describe as China's "state-coordinated investment partnerships", whereby Chinese enterprises are uniquely able to organize their overseas investments via central state support.[56] In particular, China's policy banks (the China Exim Bank and the China Development Bank) perform the crucial function of coordinating credit spaces, providing credit and loans not only to foreign host governments, but also to the Chinese firms involved—either via ownership or service provision—in such projects.[57] Unsurprisingly, then, Chinese companies gain the lion's share of construction contracts for BRI projects overseas.

A4. Classification of Industrial Sectors

In this report, four broad industrial sectors are highlighted: the infrastructure, energy, metals and others sectors. Infrastructure and energy are two industrial sectors that have featured prominently in Chinese overseas investments since the early 2000s (this is particularly the case for the infrastructure sector after the official launch of Beijing's Belt and Road Initiative in 2013). The metals sector is closely related to the infrastructure and energy sectors and has also been an important element in China's SEA investments and BRI policy (albeit not as crucial a component as the infrastructure and energy sectors). To provide a complete picture of Chinese investments by industry, we used the others sector to capture all the other industrial sectors.

We classified the aforementioned four main industrial sectors by regrouping the thirty-three industrial subsectors used in the CGIT database, as shown in Table A1.[58] Note that, subject to data limitations, including the industrial subsectors in the CGIT database being self-reported by investors, the classification of the "infrastructure" sector should best be regarded as a "best effort" to capture Chinese infrastructure investments as accurately as possible, rather than as the ultimate categorization of all Chinese infrastructure investments. Reclassifying the thirty-three industrial subsectors in the CGIT database into the four broad industrial sectors in this project also helped to avoid, at least to some extent, the sparse data issue, where data is patchy on Chinese investments in certain industrial subsectors in some SEA countries.

Table A1: Regrouping of Industrial Sectors

Four Industrial Sectors in This Project	Industrial Subsectors in the CGIT Database
Infrastructure	Construction, Telecommunications, Autos, Aviation, Rail, Shipping, Utilities
Energy	Alternative, Coal, Gas, Hydropower, Oil, Other Energy
Metals	Aluminium, Copper, Steel, Other Metals
Others	Agriculture, Chemicals, Entertainment, Banking, Investment, Other Finance, Health, Logistics, Property, Other Technology, Tourism, Consumer, Education, Industry, Textiles, Timber

A5. Main Reasons for Data Discrepancies: CGIT Database vs ASEAN Statistical Yearbooks

Data discrepancies between the CGIT database and ASEAN Statistical Yearbooks can mostly be explained by variations in how "investments" are defined, how "Chinese" is defined, and how data is collected (as detailed in Table A2). Other factors, such as investments in certain industrial sectors being excluded from data compilation in some SEA countries, also likely contribute to data discrepancies.

The following three examples illustrate how the factors outlined in Table A2 can result in data discrepancies between the CGIT database and ASEAN Statistical Yearbooks. Note that the following explanations constitute our "best guesses" based on available information. For example, these explanations could not be confirmed by the ASEAN Secretariat because data submitted by member states are aggregated and the Secretariat was unable to seek further details about individual data points.

Table A2: Variations in Definitions and Data Collection

Main Reasons	CGIT Database	ASEAN Statistical Yearbooks
Definition of "Investments"		
Monetary threshold	≥ US$100 million[1]	No requirement
Ownership threshold	> 0% ownership in the target enterprise/project[2]	≥ 10% voting power in the direct investment enterprise[3]
Definition of "Chinese"[4]		
Geo-allocation principle	Ultimate parent company	Immediate investing country[5]
Data Collection		
Method	Aggregation of cross-border investment transactions[6]	Directional principle and/or Asset/liability principle[7]
Timing	Data is recorded when the investment has been disclosed or based on the date given in the disclosure[8]	Data is recorded when the investment has flowed into the host country.

Notes:

1. Considering that the CGIT database captures Chinese investments worth at least US$100 million rather than Chinese investments of all values, due caution should be exercised when interpreting trends of Chinese investments in SEA countries revealed by the CGIT database. For example, a decrease in Chinese investments in an SEA country shown by the CGIT database indicates that Chinese investments worth at least US$100 million in that host country have declined, which does not necessarily mean that overall Chinese investments (i.e., Chinese investments of all values) have dropped in that host country.

2. The CGIT database captures Chinese (a) investments, and (b) construction contracts, which are documented both separately and together in the database. Investments are considered cross-border transactions wherein Chinese entities acquire asset ownership in SEA countries (i.e., larger than 0 per cent ownership), whereas construction contracts are considered cross-border transactions wherein Chinese entities only provide services in SEA countries (i.e., no ownership). In this report, where the CGIT database is used, Chinese investments and construction contracts in SEA countries are collectively referred to as "Chinese investments".

3. Most SEA countries follow the OECD's Framework for Direct Investment Relationships, which adopts the threshold of at least 10 per cent voting power in the direct investment enterprise for identifying direct investment relationships.

4. Also see section A2 of this Appendix.

5. All the ten SEA countries except Malaysia use the "immediate investing country" as the geo-allocation principle, while Malaysia uses the "immediate parent company" as the geo-allocation principle.

6. The transaction-based data collection method means that outflows of Chinese investments from SEA countries (i.e., divestment) would not be accounted for in the CGIT database.

7. For further information about the directional principle and asset/liability principle, please see the IMF's *Balance of Payments and International Investment Position Manual, 5th edition* (BPM5), IMF's *Balance of Payments and International Investment Position Manual, 6th edition* (BPM6), and OECD's *Benchmark Definition of Foreign Direct Investment, 4th edition* (BMD4).

8. One implication is that some committed Chinese investments that are yet to flow into host countries are likely to have been included in the CGIT database, although these committed investments might be removed from the CGIT database later if these transactions have been delayed or cancelled altogether; in cases where committed investments have been delayed and therefore temporarily removed from the CGIT database, these transactions may be added back to the CGIT database with a new transaction date to reflect the late start of these transactions. In other words, Chinese investments in the CGIT database represent committed amounts rather than realized or utilized amounts.

Example 1: The Philippines—Different Geo-allocation Principles
In 2008, the State Grid Corporation of China invested US$1.58 billion to acquire 40 per cent ownership in the National Grid Corporation of the Philippines. While this investment was recorded in the CGIT database, ASEAN Statistical Yearbooks showed Chinese FDI in the Philippines in 2008 being close to US$0 (see Figure A1). This discrepancy arose possibly because this investment was made through the State Grid Corporation of China's investment arm in Hong Kong and, given the geo-allocation principle of "immediate investing country" adopted by ASEAN Statistical Yearbooks, was therefore not counted as Chinese.

Example 2: Malaysia—Different Timings of Data Collection
As shown in Figure A2, data from the CGIT database showed that Chinese investments in Malaysia reached a record high in 2015, whereas data from ASEAN Statistical Yearbooks showed that Chinese FDI in Malaysia reached its first peak in 2016. This is possibly because the very significant investment involving Chinese acquisition of 1MDB's energy assets was recorded at different time points by these two data sources. The CGIT database likely recorded this investment when it was announced in November 2015, while ASEAN Statistical Yearbooks likely recorded this investment when it was completed in March 2016.

Example 3: Brunei—Investments in Certain Industrial Sectors Not Included in Data Compilation
In 2014, Zhejiang Hengyi Group invested US$3.44 billion in Phase 1 of an oil refinery and petrochemical complex project at Pulau Muara Besar. While this investment was recorded in the CGIT database, ASEAN Statistical Yearbooks showed Chinese FDI in Brunei in 2014 being close to US$0 (see Figure A3). This is possibly because expenditure on natural resource exploration is not included in Brunei's FDI data compilation.

    Moreover, the above factors can have more significant impacts on some SEA countries than others, in turn affecting their relative

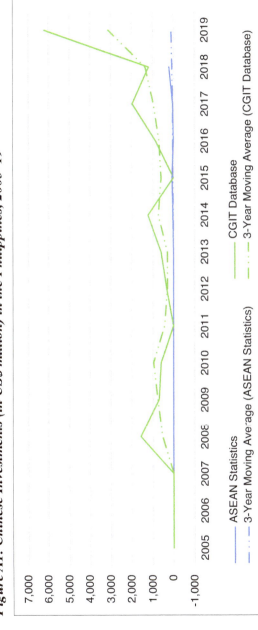

Figure A1: Chinese Investments (in US$ million) in the Philippines, 2005–19

Data Source: China Global Investment Tracker 2019 Fall Dataset (accessed in January 2020), China Global Investment Tracker 2021 Spring Dataset (accessed in August 2021), ASEAN Statistical Yearbooks.

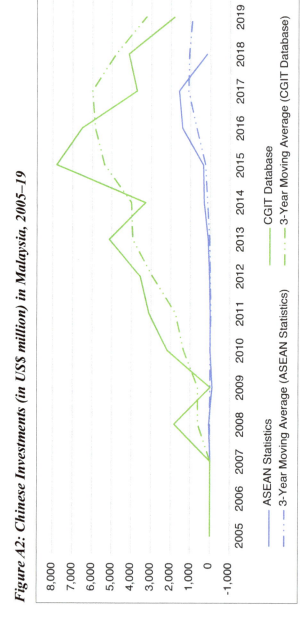

Figure A2: Chinese Investments (in US$ million) in Malaysia, 2005–19

Data Source: China Global Investment Tracker 2019 Fall Dataset (accessed in January 2020), China Global Investment Tracker 2021 Spring Dataset (accessed in August 2021), ASEAN Statistical Yearbooks.

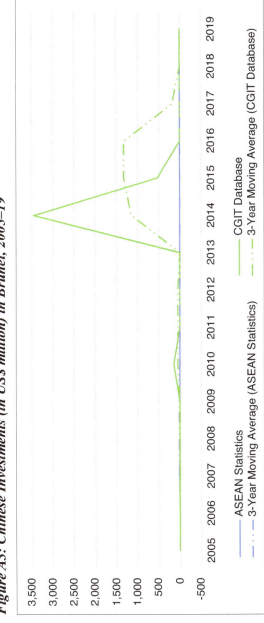

Figure A3: Chinese Investments (in US$ million) in Brunei, 2005–19

Data Source: China Global Investment Tracker 2019 Fall Dataset (accessed in January 2020), China Global Investment Tracker 2021 Spring Dataset (accessed in August 2021), ASEAN Statistical Yearbooks.

importance as destinations for Chinese investments. For example, as shown in Table A3: Malaysia had the *third largest* share of total Chinese investments in SEA according to the CGIT database, but the *third smallest* share of total Chinese FDI in SEA according to ASEAN Statistical Yearbooks. In contrast, Myanmar had the *second smallest* share of total Chinese investments in SEA according to the CGIT database but the *fourth largest* share of total Chinese FDI in SEA according to ASEAN Statistical Yearbooks. (The relative importance of the other SEA countries as destinations for Chinese investments does not vary as significantly between the CGIT database and ASEAN Statistical Yearbooks as that of Malaysia and Myanmar.)

A6. Updating Data Analysis to Incorporate New Information from the Updated CGIT Database

The CGIT database is updated biannually—once in January and once in July—to reflect new information available on Chinese overseas investments. When we first commenced our data analysis in early 2020, the final version of the CGIT 2019 fall database was the most up-to-date CGIT database available to us, and we based our preliminary analysis on that. To ensure that our final data analysis could incorporate as most recent information as possible, we used the final version of the CGIT 2021 spring database—the most up-to-date CGIT database available to us before we finalized our analysis in December 2021—to update our preliminary analysis. In updating our analysis, we needed to address two key issues:

- Whether to extend the timeframe of our analysis based on the CGIT database to the year 2020 (which was the latest year for which the CGIT 2021 spring database has full-year data on Chinese investments in SEA countries); and
- How to manage the changes between the CGIT 2019 fall database and the CGIT 2021 spring database.

Table A3: Chinese Investments in SEA Countries

CGIT Database (2005–2019)			ASEAN Statistical Yearbooks (2005–2018)		
SEA Country	Amount (in US$ million)	Share	SEA Country	Amount (in US$ million)	Share
Indonesia	53,720	21%	Singapore	40,422	52%
Singapore	46,310	18%	Indonesia	8,657	11%
Malaysia	43,060	17%	Vietnam	5,670	7%
Laos	28,650	11%	Myanmar	5,149	7%
Vietnam	25,500	10%	Laos	4,762	6%
Cambodia	16,240	6%	Cambodia	4,543	6%
Philippines	15,290	6%	Thailand	4,389	6%
Thailand	11,550	5%	Malaysia	3,839	5%
Myanmar	9,600	4%	Philippines	349	0%
Brunei	4,110	2%	Brunei	24	0%
Total	*254,030*		*Total*	*77,804*	

Data Source: China Global Investment Tracker 2019 Fall Dataset (accessed in January 2020), China Global Investment Tracker 2021 Spring Dataset (accessed in August 2021), ASEAN Statistical Yearbooks.

On the first issue, we decided to keep the original timeframe of our analysis, i.e., from 2005 to 2019, rather than extending it to the year 2020. This was primarily because we believed that the ongoing COVID-19 pandemic, as a rare and extreme event, would likely have impacts on Chinese investments in SEA countries and in this case, incorporating the 2020 data—the only full-year data available in the CGIT 2021 spring database that were subject to COVID-19 impacts—could skew the trends and patterns of Chinese investments in SEA countries since 2005 while not allowing a reasonably robust and comprehensive assessment of the potential impacts of the COVID-19 pandemic on Chinese investments in SEA countries. Instead, simply including the 2005–19 data in our analysis would allow us to present a reasonably accurate picture of the trends and patterns of Chinese investments in SEA countries prior to the COVID-19 pandemic and assist with better understanding of the key features of Chinese investments in SEA during this period. As more full-year data that has been subject to COVID-19 impacts become available in future versions of the CGIT database, we may consider further updating our analysis to extend our analysis timeframe and provide a reasonably robust assessment of the potential impacts of the COVID-19 pandemic on Chinese investments in SEA countries.

On the second issue, we classified the changes between the CGIT 2019 fall database and the CGIT 2021 spring database into three broad categories, and approached each category of changes in ways commensurate with the significance of the changes. Table A4 outlines the three broad categories of changes and the corresponding approaches to managing each category of changes.

Example 1—Melaka Gateway Port Project Undertaken by Power Construction Corp in Malaysia
This infrastructure-related construction contract transaction (valued at US$1,910 million) was recorded in 2016 in the CGIT 2019 fall database but was not captured in the CGIT 2021 spring database. We decided to remove this transaction from our analysis (i.e., in line with the CGIT 2021 spring database) because the

Table A4: Categories of Changes and Management of Changes

Category of Changes	Approaches to Changes
Any change in transactions worth *at least US$1 billion* (either such transactions in the 2019 fall dataset or such transactions in the 2021 spring dataset)	If there is publicly available information to substantiate the change reflected in the 2021 spring database, the transaction information provided in the 2021 spring database is used, to ensure that the most up-to-date information is used for the analysis (see *Example 1* above). If there is *no* publicly available information to substantiate the change reflected in the 2021 spring database, the transaction information provided in the 2019 fall database is used, given that we did not have enough evidence to verify the change (see *Example 2* below).
Any change in transactions worth *between US$500 million (inclusive) and US$1 billion (exclusive)* (either such transactions in the 2019 Fall dataset or such transactions in the 2021 Spring dataset)	If the context of the transaction (e.g., which SEA country/industry the transaction pertained to) indicates that the change would likely have a major impact on the analysis, the procedure applied to transactions worth at least US$1 billion (see below) is repeated (see *Example 3* below). If the context of the transaction indicates that the change would likely have a minor impact on the analysis, the transaction information provided in the 2021 spring database is used, to ensure that the most up-to-date information is used for the analysis.
Any change in transactions worth *less than US$500 million* (either such transactions in the 2019 Fall dataset or such transactions in the 2021 Spring dataset)	The transaction information provided in the 2021 spring database is used, to ensure that the most up-to-date information is used for the analysis.

official cancellation of the Melaka Gateway Port project was widely reported in the media.

Example 2—Thailand-China Railway Project
This infrastructure-related construction contract transaction (valued at US$2,690 million) was recorded in 2018 in the CGIT 2019 fall database but was not captured in the CGIT 2021 spring database. We decided to keep this transaction in our analysis (i.e., in line with the CGIT 2019 fall database) because despite continued delays in the commencement of this project, there did not appear to be publicly available information that could confirm the formal suspension or cancellation of this project.

Example 3—Delong Holdings Limited's Investment to Build a Steel Factory in Indonesia
This metals-related ownership acquisition transaction in 2017 was valued at US$150 million in the CGIT 2019 fall database but at US$990 million in the CGIT 2021 spring database. While the transaction amount is less than US$1 billion according to either database, the change in the transaction amount was considered to have a major impact on the analysis, as this change significantly increased Indonesia's share of total Chinese metals investments in SEA in 2017, from 17 per cent (as per the CGIT 2019 fall database) to 42 per cent (as per the CGIT 2021 spring database). Given that public information was available to confirm the US$990 million investment amount outlined in the CGIT 2021 spring database, we decided to use the US$990 million figure in our analysis (i.e., in line with the CGIT 2021 spring database).

ENDNOTES

Section 1: Overview and Analysis
1. See Shu Guang Zhang, *Beijing's Economic Statecraft during the Cold War, 1949–1991* (Baltimore: Johns Hopkins University Press, 2014).
2. We used the final version of the China Global Investment Tracker 2019 fall dataset (accessed in January 2020), the final version of the China Global Investment Tracker 2021 spring dataset (accessed in August 2021) and ASEAN Statistical Yearbooks to construct the dataset for this quantitative survey and analysis. We did not include data from 2020–21, primarily because this data was likely to have been impacted by the ongoing COVID-19 pandemic, and including this data might skew the analysis prematurely.
3. For a more detailed explanation, see section A3 of the Appendix.
4. For details about Chinese investment volumes, distribution, and projects in each country, see Section 2: Quantitative Report.
5. When agreed in 2018, the Jakarta-Bandung HSR—valued initially at US$2.5 billion—was the third most valuable Chinese infrastructure investment recorded in SEA in a single year, after the China-Laos railway project and Thailand-China railway project (also agreed in 2018). By the time of its opening in mid-2023, the HSR project cost US$7.2 billion. https://www.rfa.org/english/news/china/indonesia-china-rail-06132023125521.html
6. For example, Kuantan Port and its associated Malaysia-China Industrial Park—Kuantan is the planned southern terminal of the ECRL and these projects' (questionable) viability had been tied to two other connecting rail projects: a planned trans-peninsular rail that would connect Kuantan to the west coast via KL, and the KL-Singapore HSR.
7. See the Appendix for an explanation of the data constraints preventing us from systematically comparing foreign investments that include both ownership acquisition and service provision.
8. Between 2006 and 2018, over half of Cambodia's annual FDI came from sources outside of the top three investors, including other SEA countries.

9. Jikon Lai and Amalina Anuar, "Measures of Economic Vulnerability and Inter-Dependency in the Global Economy", *RSIS Working Paper No. 333*, 20 January 2021. Based on trade and investment flows in 2015–17, Laos, Myanmar and Cambodia were ranked 13th, 15th and 22nd respectively among the 200 countries for vulnerability to China. Other SEA economies in the top 50 were Vietnam (33rd), Malaysia (39th), Thailand (46th) and Singapore (48th).

10. Note that the coding used in this report places investments in electric companies within the energy sector, and investments in telecommunications under the infrastructure sector.

11. The two larger companies were sold to a Japanese-led consortium Lion Power and Malaysian YTL Power respectively. https://www.wsj.com/articles/SB122061029167803541; https://www.thestar.com.my/business/business-news/2008/12/03/ytl-power-acquires-powerseraya-from-temasek

12. https://www.reuters.com/article/us-temasek-huaneng-idUSSP10284220080314

13. https://www.rappler.com/nation/ph-chinese-experts-ngcp

14. On this controversial move, which some see as a debt-for-equity swap intensifying Laos' debt-trap danger, see Keith Barney and Kanya Souksakoun, "Credit Crunch: Chinese Infrastructure Lending and Lao Sovereign Debt", *Asia-Pacific Policy Studies* 8, issue 1 (2021): 94–113, https://doi-org.virtual.anu.edu.au/10.1002/app5.318

15. https://cnnphilippines.com/business/2019/4/29/Mislatel-China-Telecom.html

16. https://business.inquirer.net/260809/dennis-uy-china-telecom-venture-confirmed-as-third-telco#ixzz6nSUdJIUB

17. Melinda Martinus, "The Intricacies of 5G Development in Southeast Asia", *ISEAS Perspective*, no. 2020/130, 13 November 2020, https://www.iseas.edu.sg/wp-content/uploads/2020/11/ISEAS_Perspective_2020_130.pdf. As of October 2020, Huawei had 40 per cent share of the SEA 5G equipment market, compared to Ericsson's 20 per cent and Nokia's 15 per cent.

18. https://www.reuters.com/article/us-keppel-petrochina-idUSTRE54N13F20090525

19. http://www.xinhuanet.com/english/2020-09/17/c_139373645.htm

20. https://asia.nikkei.com/Business/Chinese-company-to-build-oil-

refinery-near-Dawei-SEZ-in-Myanmar. Project implementation has been delayed, most recently due to the COVID-19 pandemic.

21. 22 million tons—https://www.globaltimes.cn/content/1146125.shtml

22. Our calculations here are based on the stated design capacity of the gas pipeline (12 billion cubic metres per year) and the oil pipeline (22 million tons of crude oil per year); and the best data available publicly on China's total annual natural gas and crude oil imports. Note that these figures are estimates only, and liable to year-on-year changes in actual imports and in projections of China's national energy consumption. Data on China's annual natural gas and crude oil import from the Kyaukphyu pipelines is patchy and not currently verifiable.

23. Note that construction has not begun on the Dawei port, which is subject to a competing project funded by an international consortium in the SEZ; and that the Kyaukphyu port was downsized from ten to two berths after worries about a potential debt trap caused Naypyidaw to renegotiate with the Chinese-led consortium to reduce the project cost from US$7.2 billion to US$1.3 billion in 2017/8.

24. https://thediplomat.com/2020/09/sino-thai-railway-inches-toward-resumption/; https://www.railway-technology.com/news/thailand-thai-sino-high-speed/; https://www.geopoliticalmonitor.com/fact-sheet-kunming-singapore-high-speed-rail-network/

25. https://www.bangkokpost.com/thailand/general/2432925/high-speed-rail-project-behind-schedule

26. See note 37 and section A6 of the Appendix for further explanations for the chosen period of coverage. Our estimate is that once we have data to add to our dataset up to 2025, we will have the minimum basis to analyse the impacts of COVID on short-to-medium-term Chinese investment patterns.

27. One study suggests that China's overseas bailouts correspond to more than 20 per cent of total IMF lending over the past decade, with 80 per cent of China's bailouts occurring between 2016 and 2020—see S. Horn, B. Parks, C. Reinhart, and C. Trebesch, "China as an International Lender of Last Resort", Working Paper #124. (Williamsburg, VA: AidData at William & Mary, 2023), https://www.aiddata.org/publications/china-as-an-international-lender-of-last-resort

28. Note that the data in the various studies cited in this section is preliminary and, due to their method of collation, not directly comparable with the two main datasets we have drawn upon for our dataset and analysis here. See Appendix for a detailed explanation of our methodology.

29. Alicia García Herrero, "Will the Belt and Road Initiative Be Another Casualty of the Pandemic?", *Georgetown Journal of International Affairs*, 11 November 2022, https://gjia.georgetown. edu/2022/11/11/will-the-belt-and-road-initiative-be-another-casualty-of-the-pandemic/

30. See Beatrice Tanjanco et al., "China Navigates its COVID-19 Recovery—Outward Investment Appetite and Implications for Developing Countries", Overseas Development Institute Economic Pulse Series (February 2021), https://cdn.odi.org/media/documents/odi_economic_pulse_2_final12feb.pdf

31. Wang Zheng, "Assessing the Belt and Road Initiative in Southeast Asia amid the COVID-19 Pandemic", *ISEAS Perspective*, no. 2022/57, 26 May 2022, https://www.iseas.edu.sg/articles-commentaries/iseas-perspective/2022-57-assessing-the-belt-and-road-initiative-in-southeast-asia-amid-the-covid-19-pandemic-2021-2022-by-wang-zheng/

32. See, for example, Kaho Yu, "The Belt and Road Initiative in Southeast Asia after COVID-19: China's Energy and Infrastructure Investments in Myanmar", *ISEAS Perspective*, no. 2021/39, 6 April 2021, https://www.iseas.edu.sg/articles-commentaries/iseas-perspective/2021-39-the-belt-and-road-initiative-in-southeast-asia-after-covid-19-chinas-energy-and-infrastructure-investments-in-myanmar-by-kaho-yu/

33. See ERIA, *The COVID-19 Pandemic: Impact on ASEAN Connectivity and Recovery Strategies* (2022), https://www.oecd.org/southeast-asia/ERIA%20COVID19%20and%20ASEAN%20Connectivity.pdf

34. This is an aim that is in line with some data suggesting that the Asian Development Bank and the World Bank overtook China as the leading sources of foreign investment in Southeast Asia in 2021. See "New Lowy South-East Asia Aid Map Finds China Overtaken as Largest Provider of Development Money in Region", *ABC News*, 5 June 2023, https://www.abc.net.au/news/2023-06-05/lowy-south-east-asia-foreign-aid-map/102414992?utm_

source=abc_news_web&utm_medium=content_shared&utm_
campaign=abc_news_web

Section 2: Quantitative Report

35. See Appendix for how "Chinese investments" are defined in the CGIT database and ASEAN Statistical Yearbooks. In this report, we use the phrase "Chinese investments" when the analysis draws on data from CGIT, and "Chinese FDI" when data from ASEAN Statistical Yearbooks is used.

36. The analysis started from 2005 primarily because we want to present a comprehensive analysis of the rapid development of China's outward direct investments since the early 2000s, after the "Going Global" strategy was initiated by the Chinese government in 1999, and relevant datasets that would allow us to conduct this analysis have been generally available for the period since 2005.

37. The analysis did not include data from 2020, primarily because the 2020 data were likely to have been impacted by the ongoing COVID-19 pandemic and including this data might skew the analysis prematurely. UNCTAD noted that the impact of the pandemic on global foreign direct investment was strongest in the first half of 2020, and that in the second half of the year, "cross-border mergers and acquisitions and international project finance deals largely recovered". However, greenfield investment—which UNCTAD notes is more important for developing countries— "continued its negative trend throughout 2020 and into the first quarter of 2021". Looking ahead, UNCTAD expected that global foreign direct investment flows would bottom out in 2021 and recover some lost ground, with an increase of about 10 to 15 per cent. But this would still leave levels "some 25 per cent below the 2019 level".

38. https://www.oecd.org/daf/inv/investmentstatisticsandanalysis/40193734.pdf

39. ASEAN Statistical Yearbooks were used when assessing the relative importance of Chinese investments in SEA countries. The Appendix provides more detailed explanations of why ASEAN Statistical Yearbooks were used alongside the CGIT dataset, and data discrepancies between ASEAN Statistical Yearbooks and the CGIT dataset.

40. See section A4 of the Appendix for detailed discussions about why

the four sectors (i.e., infrastructure, energy, metals and others) were chosen and how these sectors were categorized.

41.   Timor-Leste is not considered in the scope of this report.

42.   Based on CGIT data. Note that the top three destinations and their respective shares might be slightly different if other datasets were used.

43.   The CGIT database captures Chinese (a) investments, and (b) construction contracts, which are documented both separately and together in the database. Investments are considered cross-border transactions wherein Chinese entities acquire asset ownership in SEA countries (i.e., larger than 0 per cent ownership), whereas construction contracts are considered cross-border transactions wherein Chinese entities only provide services in SEA countries (i.e., no ownership). In this report, where the CGIT database is used, Chinese investments and construction contracts in SEA countries are collectively referred to as "Chinese investments".

44.   In assessing the relative importance of Chinese investments in SEA countries, we drew on data from the ASEAN Statistical Yearbooks. Given ASEAN Statistical Yearbooks and the CGIT dataset adopt different methodologies for compiling Chinese investment data, discrepancies on the amounts of Chinese investments in SEA countries can be observed. The data discrepancy appears to be more significant for some SEA countries, especially Malaysia. The Appendix provides more detailed explanations of these data discrepancies, and why two different data sources were used for this report.

45.   This project was scrapped by the Melaka government in late November 2020, reportedly because the developer had failed to complete the reclamation works after three years as contracted. Because of the official cancellation of this project, this investment was not captured in the CGIT 2021 Spring dataset we used for this report and therefore not reflected in the figures/tables and other statistics we presented in this report. Source: https://www. straitstimes.com/asia/se-asia/melaka-state-govt-scraps-14-billion-port-project

46.   This project was cancelled in September 2012, about half a year after the investment agreement was reached. Source: https:// www.thestar.com.my/news/nation/2012/09/08/johor-sultan-says-mersing-laguna-project-cancelled

47. This US$1.58 billion investment did not appear to have been recorded in ASEAN Statistical Yearbooks (see the Appendix for possible reasons), which seemed to have affected the relative importance of Chinese FDI in the Philippines in 2008 (see Table 14).

48. This US$3.44 billion investment did not appear to have been recorded in ASEAN Statistical Yearbooks (see the Appendix for possible reasons), which seemed to have affected the relative importance of Chinese FDI in Brunei in 2014 (see Table 17).

Appendix

49. For example, the World Bank does not provide country-to-country FDI data; China's Bureau of Statistics outward FDI data does not cover every SEA country; and the China Global Energy Finance database only covers various energy-related investments.

50. We first accessed the CGIT database in January 2020 and initially only used the final version of the 2019 fall database for our data analysis. While we were working on our data analysis, the CGIT database was periodically updated to reflect new information available. To ensure that our final analysis could also reflect the new information available, we incorporated the final version of the CGIT 2021 spring database (which was the most recent CGIT database available to us before we finalized our analysis in December 2021) into our preliminary analysis, which was based on the final version of the CGIT 2019 fall database. Section A6 of this Appendix provides more details on how we updated our preliminary analysis using the most recent CGIT database available to us.

51. Further information about the CGIT database is available on its website: https://www.aei.org/china-global-investment-tracker/

52. Further information about ASEAN Statistical Yearbooks is available on its website: https://www.aseanstats.org/category/yearbook/

53. Given that the ASEAN Statistical Yearbooks do not capture cross-border transactions that only involve service provision (i.e. no acquisition of ownership) by investing countries, the relative importance of Chinese investments in a SEA country, when measured by the data from the ASEAN Statistical Yearbooks, might be underestimated in circumstances where (1) Chinese investments in the form of service provision were concentrated in a few years rather than being spread across the whole period of 2005–18; and

(2) Chinese investments in the form of service provision were quite large. Vietnam is a case in point: More than 60 per cent of Chinese service provision in Vietnam during 2005–18 was concentrated in 2009–12, and the annual amount of Chinese service provision in Vietnam during 2009–12 was also quite large (at approximately US$2.5 billion to US$4 billion per year). In this case, the relative importance of Chinese investments in Vietnam during 2009–12, as measured by the data from the ASEAN Statistical Yearbooks, might be underestimated.

54.   We accessed ASEAN Statistical Yearbooks in February to April 2020 and used *ASEAN Statistical Yearbook 2008* for relevant FDI data from 2005 to 2008 and *ASEAN Statistical Yearbook 2019* for relevant FDI data from 2009 to 2018. While *ASEAN Statistical Yearbook 2020*, which contains data on FDI inflows into SEA countries in 2019, was published in December 2020—before we finalized our data analysis, we noted that *ASEAN Statistical Yearbook 2020* does not include the 2019 data on FDI inflows into SEA countries by major source country, and were advised by ASEAN Secretariat that these data were not produced for *ASEAN Statistical Yearbook 2020*—nor would these data be provided separately—due to confidential issues in some ASEAN member states. As a result, we were unable to extend our analysis that was based on ASEAN Statistical Yearbooks to the year 2019, to align with the timeframe that we used for our analysis based on the CGIT database (i.e., 2005 to 2019).

55.   United National Conference on Trade and Development, *World Investment Report 2020: International Production Beyond the Pandemic* (New York: United Nations, 2020), p. 18.

56.   R. Gonzalez-Vicente, "Make Development Great Again? Accumulation Regimes, Spaces of Sovereign Exception and the Elite Development Paradigm of China's Belt and Road Initiative", *Business and Politics* 21, no. 4 (2019): 487–513.

57.   For example, G.T. Chin and K.P. Gallagher, "Coordinated Credit Spaces: The Globalization of Chinese Development Finance", *Development and Change* 50, issue 1 (2019): 245–74.

58.   For the CGIT database, the industrial subsector to which a Chinese investment belongs is self-reported by the investor, indicating that there appears to be no specific rule for matching a Chinese investment with an industrial subsector.

INDEX